MY RIGHT TO PLAY

A Child with Complex Needs

Debating Play Series

Series Editor: Tina Bruce

The intention behind the Debating Play series is to encourage readers to reflect on their practice so that they are in a position to offer high quality play opportunities to children. The series will help those working with young children and their families in diverse ways and contexts, to think about how to cultivate early childhood play with rich learning potential.

The Debating Play series examines cultural myths and taboos. It considers matters of human rights and progress towards inclusion in the right to play for children with complex needs. It looks at time honoured practices and argues for the removal of constraints on emergent play. It challenges readers to be committed to promoting play opportunities for children traumatised through war, flight, violence and separation from loved ones. The series draws upon crucial contemporary research which demonstrates how children in different parts of the world develop their own play culture in ways which help them to make sense of their lives.

Published and forthcoming titles

Holland: *We Don't Play With Guns Here*
Hyder: *War, Conflict and Play*
Kalliala: *Play Culture in a Changing World*
Manning-Morton: *A Time to Play: Playing, growing and learning in the first three   years of life*
Orr: *My Right to Play: A Child with Complex Needs*

MY RIGHT TO PLAY

A Child with Complex Needs

Robert J. Orr

Open University Press
Maidenhead · Philadelphia

Open University Press
McGraw-Hill Education
McGraw-Hill House
Shoppenhangers Road
Maidenhead
Berkshire
England
SL6 2QL

email: enquiries@openup.co.uk
world wide web: www.openup.co.uk

and

325 Chestnut Street
Philadelphia, PA 19106, USA

First published 2003

A catalogue record of this book is available from the British Library

ISBN 0 335 21170 4 (pb)   0 335 21171 2 (hb)

Library of Congress Cataloging-in-Publication Data
Orr, Robert J., 1942–
    My right to play : a child with complex needs / Robert J. Orr
        p. cm. – (Debating play)
    Includes bibliographical references and index.
    ISBN 0–335–21171–2 – ISBN 0–335–21170–4 (pbk.)
    1. Children with disabilities – Development. I. Title. II. Series.

HV894 .O77 2003
362.1'9892' – dc21

2002035506

Typeset by RefineCatch Limited, Bungay, Suffolk
Printed in Great Britain by Bell and Bain Ltd, Glasgow

Dedicated to the memory of David Preston, to that marvel of educated womanhood, Meryal, and to our children Rachel Lovell, Toby and Nathan Orr. Also to Zak and Hannah Lovell, in case they ever wonder what Grandpa did apart from mow their lawn.

CONTENTS

SERIES EDITOR'S INTRODUCTION

The Debating Play series is not intended to make comfortable reading. This is because 'play' is not a comfortable subject. For a century at least, play has been hotly debated among researchers, practitioners, parents, politicians and policy makers. Arguments have centred around whether it should have a place in any childhood curriculum framework. Its presence in schools and other institutions and settings has ebbed and flowed according to who holds power, influence and authority to control curriculum decisions.

When play has been permitted in settings, it has often suffered from a work/play divide. Play in such contexts is frequently confused with recreation. However, an alternative approach is to offer 'free play', through which children are thought to learn naturally. This works well in mixed age groups (2–7 years) when older, more experienced child players act as tutors and initiate younger children, helping them to learn through their play. Sadly, though, this is rarely experienced in early childhood settings in the UK nowadays. It is noteworthy, however, that a few nursery schools have managed, against great odds, to keep an age range from 3–5 years and research indicates that the learning children do through their play in these settings is rich.

There is a growing understanding of the importance of play as diverse evidence accrues, which highlights the role of play in early learning in relation to ideas, feelings, relationships and movement (embodiment). However, this is often mistakenly interpreted as adults showing children how to play, through guiding, tutoring, role-modelling or whatever name is of current fashion, rather than providing children with genuine opportunities to engage in their *own* play.

The intention behind the Debating Play series is to encourage readers to reflect on their practice so that they are in a position to offer high quality play opportunities to children. The series will help those working with young children and their families in diverse ways and contexts, to think about how to cultivate early childhood play with rich learning potential.

The Debating Play series examines cultural myths and taboos (such as weapon and super hero play). It considers matters of human rights and progress towards inclusion in the right to play for children with complex needs. It looks at time honoured practices and argues for the removal of constraints on emergent play. It challenges readers to be committed to promoting play opportunities for children traumatized through war, flight, violence and separation from loved ones. The series draws upon crucial contemporary research which demonstrates how children in different parts of the world develop their own play culture in ways which help them to make sense of their lives.

The Debating Play series is evidence-based rather than belief driven. *My Right to Play: A Child with Complex Needs* is the sort of book that will engage you so deeply that you will miss your stop and fail to alight from the train at your intended destination.

Robert Orr, through the eyes of one child, helps readers to apply 'theory of mind', sharing his practical wisdom and theoretical understanding in a form that enables others to work sensitively and with responsiveness, all the while drawing upon an evidence base.

Robert Orr has worked with children who have complex needs for many years as both headteacher of a special needs school and Multi-disability Visual Impairment Training Officer with the Royal National Institute for the Blind. He has promoted the pioneer work of Lilli Nielsen in the UK and helped practitioners to move from a deficit model of disability to one of inclusion.

When I invited Robert Orr to write a book in the Debating Play series, I knew that he would, in a unique way, shed light on how we can give children with complex needs the right to play. He has succeeded masterfully in this.

Tina Bruce
Series Editor

PREFACE

These episodes serve to illustrate some of the main principles in understanding the development and needs of a person with multiple disabilities. The book is designed to be read by both families and workers, either as a story, or as a source of technical information when the standard academic texts seem too daunting. It contains examples of effective and ineffective ways of intervening, with comments by the author on how the experiences can be seen as educational, though not easily related to current curricular approaches. The child in the story is a composite of hundreds of children who had no voice to declare their perspective on life and little power to shape their own lives had it not been for well-informed and sensitive carers. The focus is on the early years and the need for play but contains material relevant to all age groups and a variety of specialists – therapists and medics, educators and social carers – and parents, who have to be all of these.

INTRODUCTION

Like other authors who set out to speak in a collective other's voice and those who dare to speak from a disabled person's point of view while not themselves being disabled, I take the fiction writer's way out, not through cowardice or laziness, but to find an authentic tone which says that this is what some people experience. Peter Carey's *The Unusual Life of Tristan Smith* (1994), which speaks from the perspective of a child with 'multiple congenital anomalies' or Thomas and Znaniecki's *The Polish Peasant* (1996), and Isaac Bashevis Singer's *Crown of Feathers* (1973), spring to mind as legitimisers of this approach.

For this work I lean partly on the notes that the late David Preston and I made about his life and schooling and I have now completed the task he charged me with when he was dying of cancer of the throat: 'Get that bloomin' book written'. This resembles the cry my editor Tina Bruce has often taken up, and she has urged my wife Meryal to do the same.

David went to an RNIB Sunshine House School at the age of 4 in the middle of the last century and remembered with disbelief the number of tiny babies who were there merely because they were blind, and the rare parental visits his peers received in the long terms with no half-term break. His own mother (whom he referred to as 'the loud and Scottish') maintained a regular pattern of fortnightly visits against the trend. She had given birth to him prematurely in a caravan in Scotland far from services; his blindness and disabilities were partly due to that prematurity and partly to the incubator treatment that was the only treatment then available.

David could reproduce whole conversations in the voices of the people concerned from that early school period near Shrewsbury and he remembers one of his peers who was taken to Leamington Spa Sunshine House as a baby who later could recall the conversations he heard during his admission, held in his father's arms, even though this was before the child himself could speak.

As a radio journalist, David visited his old school at RNIB Rushton Hall when I had become the head teacher there. We discovered a common interest in things educational and philosophical, things political and things associated with real ale. We remained at variance over things religious. He joined me on a committee of parents who had created Vision Homes Association which provides domestic support and places to live for people who have impaired vision and other disabilities. He argued with anyone up for a discussion on life, its meanings and definitions. He agreed he had spasticity and blindness but would not agree that he suffered from them. He was a spirited advocate of his own rights and those of other disabled people, especially on behalf of those who could not articulate them for themselves.

At his memorial service at the Torch Trust, close to his home in Leicestershire, a tape of his failing voice was played in which he said that if the first thing he saw when he died was his Saviour's face, then he would be content.

I offer this text in his memory and in the fervent hope that people working with clients and students with complex needs will make sounder judgements in providing support for people who, but for their disabilities, would not need it and that families who read it will take a few short cuts in arriving at ways of accommodating their children's needs.

Such families sometimes find themselves isolated and ill-prepared for the lifestyle changes that confront their familiar social landscape. In these days of inclusion, the old concentrations of know-how in special schools and specialist services are, for good reason, rarer and the opportunities for newcomers to acquire skills from experienced people and to meet those facing similar issues are consequently less. I worked among people who struggled to come to an understanding of what was appropriate and now I pass on some of the things they came up with at Rushton and all the other national and international places I visited as a trainer and colleague in the multiple disability, visual impairment field. About 110 children with compound disabilities and visual impairment 'passed through my hands' between 1979 and 1991 and I encountered hundreds more in my training role from then to 1999.

I hope all those workers and parents will accept my generalized thanks for being generous with their discoveries and knowledge and will enjoy spotting themselves in this fictionalized account.

My special thanks to Professor Tina Bruce for all her encouragement and support and to Penny Holland for suggesting to Tina that the work should be divided into episodes.

My 'off the wall' column in the RNIB journal *Eye Contact* was the testing ground for some of the following. The errors and distortions contained herein are, of course, my own but the good stuff is to the credit of the gifted people who inspired me to collect and relay their stories.

David and I had a working title for this project – 'A Kind of Living': may you, the reader, live long and prosper!

Episode 1

MY SECURE BASE

I was never what you would call a well baby. Is that a new term? Not all was well with me. My first few weeks were spent in an incubator. At home, when I was quiet, my mother used to think it meant I was fine but actually I was running out of things to do and would kind of shut down. Occasionally I'd lie still at people to convince them I wanted them to engage with me but no one seemed to pick up my 'I'm-being-still-to-get-you' signal.

The main advantage of being still is that you can tell better who's around.

Attentiveness and shutting down are two very different stillnesses. One is purposeful, the other listless. Only my sister seemed to understand the difference and she was too little to explain to the big ones quite what my different stillnesses meant. She used to say 'OK, I'll leave you in peace, but I'll be back in a couple of minutes' (though sometimes she'd forget and would start up some activity that took her mind off me) but sometimes she'd say things like 'Yes, it is a strange noise, isn't it? It's a lorry outside the shop opposite. The man's unloading biscuits.'

Sometimes she knew it wasn't listening that I was doing attentively but that I was trying to work out where the draught was coming from or what that smell was. She often knew when I was too hot, too cold, or bored and lonely and she'd snuggle up to me and wriggle around a lot. That always cheered me up no end.

Children who don't use sight as their main means of studying events out there are often described in the literature as 'stilling' in response to stimuli.

Dad at that time was really nervous about me and picked me up as if I might break in his hands but he got better as I got tougher and eventually sat me on his shoulders for some outings.

I remember the first time he stuffed me in his rucksack contraption and went up an escalator in a department store. He thought I'd wet myself from fear until he saw my face and realized I was excited and had momentarily lost bladder control with the thrill of it all!

> Patricia Sonksen and her team at the Wolfson Centre described rough and tumble as 'father play' and observed that the more disabled children are the less they get thrown about. This may be an essential part of a child's early experience and assist in the development of the sense of balance controlled from the vestibular organ in the inner ear. There is a fascinating account of factors which might delay a complex child's development in Sonksen *et al.* (1984).

It was my father's father who noticed how I would throw myself around in the old zinc laundry bath as a play space and it was he who first tied baby toys to the edge to dangle inside for me to dabble with. But it was Grandma who said bits of old plastic were no good for me and put all sorts of really useful things in.

She had been reading about my kind of play needs and had collected metal utensils with wobbly ends and wooden handles and even sacrificed the ancestral spurtle [a turned wooden rod] that her grandmother had stirred porridge with. I've never come across another one since and sometimes rub my thumb against my finger as a way of remembering the feel of that wood that was heavy with Celtic cookery sensations reverberating in its shaft. It is still a favourite memory of mine to help me unwind and get to sleep after a frustrating day. For years I clung onto pieces of wood and rejected cuddly toys, much to many people's consternation.

The other associated memory is of the floor of the tin bath and its sides. I would finger the objects and rub my back on the reverberating floor and press my feet against the handle end. I would also be put in a huge basket to play and I felt the way strands of my hair got tangled in the weave so that when Mum lifted me out I would leave bits of me behind.

> The Danish special educator Dr Lilli Nielsen *R* (the R indicates that she became a Dame in the 2001 Danish new year's honours list) writes entertainingly about her work on small acoustic spaces

for blind children, the 'Little Room'. Her book *Space and Self* describes for the general reader her research into the increased activity of otherwise passive children once they are elevated on a resonant platform and enclosed in a hard-walled space full of enticing materials. Her PhD was on blind babies reaching out and is available from the RNIB: *Spatial Relations in Congenitally Blind Infants* (1988), written in English.

Come to think of it, being lifted up was often like leaving bits of me behind. So sudden was the acceleration that I felt as if I was trailing debris. My aunt Sue had the best lift. She would rub my ribs before grabbing me and then lift me to her knees with a 'hup' sound, then to her thighs, belly and breast before hoisting me over her shoulder to nuzzle me with her cheek and scrub me gently with her hair.

Sudden contact can be overwhelming to a child who has not seen you approach. Full contact, so often necessary in the care of such people, can be made less intolerable by phasing in or building up from unthreatening touch. A moment resting against the child's foot or knee while explaining what will happen next can wipe out startle reflexes and ease transitions from one state to another.

I remember discovering one summer that my mother's sister had toes and that she was fatter than my mum but on a similar scale. I remember the awful pong of uncle Tim's tobacco-sodden beard and the knotty muscles on his forearms all bristling with hairs. He used to have me in hysterics when he hummed, *basso profundo*, onto the back of my neck. Maybe it was he who showed my dad that it was all right to be boisterous with me. He could get me and my sister under the same arm and have us gasping for breath and wriggling to escape, only to be caught up again.

I was 19 the last time he hoisted me onto his hip. He flung me into a ballpool in a motorway service station. He shouted 'Equal access for all' and dived in on top of me. The security staff made him get out and helped get me back onto my wheels. They weren't amused at his declaration that too much of a good thing can be wonderful. Someone on another table tut-tutted at us and my uncle's whole body coiled for action but all he said was 'tut-tut yourself', which I think showed remarkable restraint.

My teacher reckoned she could empty a motorway service station restaurant in six minutes flat, just by arriving with her little brood. Joe Public is an unpredictable chap. There was a time when my carers used to carry a little card so that if people tried to engage them in conversation while one of us was wrecking a joint, or just being there, they could slip them a little information about who we were, what we were doing and who they could phone if they wanted further information. It got one of my helpers out of a spot of bother when a friend of mine was hanging onto his hair screaming and we were about to be taken to the police station on suspicion of child abuse (more like staff abuse on this occasion).

That day at the restaurant, my uncle also complained about the tables and chairs all being bolted to the floor in clusters so that I couldn't get to the table. Good job my parents weren't there; they'd have died of embarrassment!

He spooned a cappuccino into me which he had done about three times a year for the last 15 years. One day I'll tell him that he needn't demand extra chocolate for me, but I don't want to upset him – and does he really think three sugars are necessary? He always nudges me and calls it his special treat and does it so that Sue can pretend she hasn't noticed him doing it. Journeys would be dull without these episodes.

Journeys have always puzzled and sometimes annoyed me. Especially when people forget to tell me where we're going. I went through a patch when I'd kick up a stink about minibuses. It all came from an occasion when I was whisked away from my nursery without warning in one such bus and never went back. For a long time afterwards I was convinced each time I got in a minibus that this was the end of my time at wherever I was being taken from. One of my teachers cracked it and always said where we were going and that we would then come back. I could relax and enjoy the trip much better then.

My escort thought she had discovered a new disability: the inability to get in and out of minibuses. An Australian pal of mine acquired this disability by stretching her arms and legs out wide so that she could not be posted in through the hole. Not bad for a kid who showed no understanding of posting boxes and scored zilch on most Piagetian tests. She had a psychologist desensitizing her to her fear of minibuses until someone with a different stance suggested she was avoiding going to school. She used to arrive late during this period with her mum deceiving her into getting into the car on some pretext other than going to school.

I was there in the room when she uttered her first words in 13 years. As a baby she had talked, but after her eyes had been removed because of the pain of glaucoma, she woke up from the operation with her hands tied to stop her picking at the bandages and said 'What have they done to my hands?' That was the last thing she said until a peripatetic teacher was playing with an enormous builder's muck bucket which she put over her head and rattled marbles on. The girl said 'What has she put on my head?' This is not a very remarkable thing to say but it is remarkable to wait 13 years to say it! She was eventually transferred to a specialist school for blind children with multiple disabilities and achieved a remarkable spontaneous recovery from the getting-into-minibuses disability. My teacher sometimes told people she was an elective mute and confused a few people until she translated it into English for non-speech and language therapists (like me) as being able to speak but choosing not to.

There was one woman who, like most people then, thought I didn't understand speech and used to roll up my towel and costume and insist that it stayed on my lap all the way to the pool so that I would know where I was going. I thought she was daft but, one day, I nodded off in the bus, woke up in a panic, felt the towel on my lap and realized what was going on.

My sister always had her swimming togs in a drawstring bag and always had the same towel with her name on it – I used to think it would be nice to have my own even though any old towel gets you dry the same.

It was at the pool that the towel woman made a breakthrough. I've never forgotten it and have never been able to thank her (I've never been able to thank anybody formally). She was manoeuvring me into a shower and offered me two shampoos to choose from. This had never happened before. I was stumped for a moment, but she unscrewed the tops and let me smell them. One was rosemary and I didn't fancy smelling of that all day so I went for the pine one. She noticed me stiffen my legs and jaw and took that as a positive choice. To prove to her I meant it I opted for rosemary the next week and spent all day smelling like a herb garden just to make a point. I was going to tell her that I smelt better than Rosemary in our class but couldn't work out a way of telling her.

Judith Coupe-O'Kane and Judith Goldbart (1998) encourage us to take any movement as a potentially communicative act so that a child can come to realize that movements can be used as intentional communications. These are likely to be unique to the individual who is at a pre-intentional stage but possibly can be developed later into an orthodox sign system. *Communication Before Speech*, 2nd edn, has their Affective Communication Schedule which maps out the areas of the body that might be active in response to any given stimulus; these movements need to be observed and used as if they were signals.

Granny had a sister with a weird accent which I eventually learned was Geordie. She always referred to me as 'the bairn' which had me confused for ages. It was she who first brought one of my disabilities to my attention. She used to get all morbid. Once she actually wept beside me, saying 'If only those little eyes could see!' It came at a good time because I had just embarked on a study of why it was that people knew, and could do, all sorts of magical things that had me completely flummoxed.

Most of my ideas about other people were fragmentary or disjointed and I had been piecing together the puzzle of how my wheelchair got me from one place to another – even in unfamiliar surroundings, so my great-aunt's distressed remark slotted a few more clues into place; in fact it was a key piece which joined various parts up. I began to fathom out how people could see and I could not. I'm no great expert on vision but I do have some notion of how it works. Some things defeat me still – like how sighted people can see huge things through a tiny window. I know it has something to do with perspective and O level physics, but that particular set of information has never been on offer in my curriculum. I'm still 'working towards Level 1', they tell me, and I probably always shall, the rate they're going!

I first discovered what a whole wheelchair was like when a teacher hung one over me so I could explore it by banging it and knocking its wheels round. I'd been sitting in one for yonks but had never gained an impression of how it all worked. This helped a bit, having another angle of it to explore.

- A quiet child might be an attentive child.
- Children need rough and tumble to keep them healthy.
- Small acoustic spaces are great to play in.

Episode 2

A SENSE OF TIME

It might help if I put my story in some sort of time sequence but my memory system, if it qualifies as a system, can be erratic and flits across decades faster than Star Trek's *Enterprise*.

I had a system at school that helped me structure time and understand the sequence of events in the timetable. Life isn't like that though; associations trigger vivid memories unconnected in a time sense and occasionally I am convinced that dreams are the same as other events. It's all grist to my mill but I'll order it in as digestible a way as I can for you.

Take that school system for instance. It may not have been early in my life but it did represent the birth of something significant. Mainly it was used to tyrannize me, to help me anticipate what I was going to be forced to do against my wishes or in accordance with them. Either way the system was a representation of things I was not consulted on which I would be introduced to at times and in ways which were beyond my control but in somebody else's.

My teacher found a way of getting a quoit into my grasp and used to say 'Circle Time' and move me to any old place on the central carpet and make me wait for ages before I was introduced to the class (either that or someone else had to wait ages). It always baffled me why this was necessary as I'd heard them all come into the classroom and they'd all registered the fact that I was present, mostly because of my escort's irritating laugh.

So Circle Time followed the presentation of a little rubber ring. My teacher thought I would come to associate the cue with Circle Time, and I did pretty soon. I remember contorting my jaw in an attempt to say 'Oh no, not bloomin' circle time', and the teacher used to say 'Good holding, yes it's circle time, your favourite.'

If only my great-aunt had intoned 'If only those little hands could hold' maybe I would have realized sooner that it was spasticity that got in the way at times like this and that most kids could throw quoits whereas I crushed them in my grip, which wasn't really my grip at all but a spasm I could neither close nor release on demand. And it wasn't just my hands. My voice used to behave like it wasn't mine too.

Speakers nearly all responded as if I had said something when some of my cries were about as meaningful as one of my not infrequent belches.

I have a vicious right hook. Once again it is stretching a point to say that it was I who had it since it seemed not to be part of me at all; it was actually owned by my cerebral palsy which I blame for most of the trouble I get into to this day.

> The Spastics Society, now Scope, once ran a novel advertisement that pointed out that the normal occurrence of cerebral palsy in a population is 0.2%. It is therefore normal to have cerebral palsy. Nice logic!

If someone is tall and thin I can actually lift them off the floor with a deft sweep to the groin. They have to struggle off my left bicep as if they were astride a bike, as one of the more communicative of them once told me.

The first time I encountered a Little Room was at an exhibition and my teacher got hold of one on loan. She used to fill it with all sorts of things for me to whack. Once she left me out of the literacy hour which the whole class is supposed to do, and hung various stationery objects around me. There was a very satisfactory pencil case which clonked resonantly as I kicked it with my left foot and a reporter's notebook for my right foot to conjure with. There were felt-tip pens by my left ear and a ruler which got in the way of my left hand. I found myself very entertaining on that day, especially when I got a pencil sharpener in my mouth and found it would whistle when I breathed out!

> The Little Room is about a meter cubed, made of interlocking poles and panels that clip onto it. It is manufactured in Sweden and goes with a resonansplatform which has to be home-made. There is a new simple-to-erect version available on the net. The kneehole of a desk would probably serve as well in the meantime.

In a nutshell
- Objects and movements associated with an activity have communication potential.
- There isn't usually enough for a blind child to do. Hang lots of things around them so they cannot lose them and get frustrated.

Episode 3

A SENSE OF PLACE

I had a very small world at one time. I sort of existed around my face where I could smell and hear and feel my world. Anything further away from me would fade into non-existence and startle me when it appeared or reappeared.

Trudy, a visiting special needs teacher, taught me one important lesson with a simple process she invented on the spur of the moment.

We had been fiddling with bits on my tray, her usual assortment of strange hardware she toted around in her bag for kids like me. One of the pegs she'd been clipping to an unused paint tin slipped off the tray and into the void (or onto the floor as sighted people tend to call it). Trudy bent down and snapped it open and shut so that I could hear where it was. As usual it had landed on a carpet so I hadn't heard where it had gone (and might not have connected the sound of it landing with a falling peg anyway). She rattled it against the front wheel of my chair and dragged it up the frame and my leg and body so that it emerged nearer the world of my face from a known route.

It was one of those 'Aha!' moments when another penny dropped. I expanded my world to the foot of my chair, beyond even my own feet. Those feet seemed remote and unimportant to me at that time and I hadn't found out how to use them for anything much but flailing about. I use them quite a bit now for searching for things and for occasional signs.

We had some fun making a video of signs in our class and we were doing 'same as'. My helper was holding out my forefingers and banging them together while most of the others managed unassisted. When the staff watched the replay one of them noticed that I was banging my feet together. Since that day they have been better at looking beyond my face and hands for communication. They eventually cottoned on to me waggling my left foot for 'no thank you' and we eventually got round to tapping them together as a request for more of the same. I forget how that developed from 'same as' but they found I could reliably produce this movement on all but my weirdest days when nothing much will do as I want it to.

I can usually tell in the morning if I have seized up and sometimes I can persuade Mum to keep me off school. I know I won't be much good there and do hate those switched-off days when I find everything and everybody mildly irritating. They usually nag me kindly with remarks like 'Come on, I know you can do this, we did it last week and I ticked it off on your card.'

There's one fellow who likes taking me outside; I think he's on some sort of trainee scheme. He can spot my off days and volunteers to take me for a stroll around the school playing fields. The best thing is he doesn't bother me much with too much detail, just leaves me to soak up what I can and doze off if I want to. His roll-ups have that sort of smell that stays with him all day and helps me identify him. I'm not sure it would count as value for money on an Ofsted inspection but I do appreciate low-input days.

Talking of Ofsted! Now there's a pantomime. My teacher was going to blow a gasket during our first one. I was convinced they were going to cart her off to the funny farm at one point. She couldn't remember my name by the third day they were observing her but the forces of good were on form and the heating system failed so we all had to go home for one of the days. I sometimes wonder whether someone didn't sabotage it deliberately, or does fate sometimes play good tricks as well as bad?

My uncle says life's a lottery and I got a dud ticket. He's a bit gloomy sometimes and he unburdens all his worries when we're alone together. I'd quite like to be a counsellor. If I could only say 'Uh-hu' at the right moments I could make a fortune. Our school psychologist is from the Uh-hu school of counselling, she says. I'm sure I could earn my living doing that.

My uncle says I'm the only person he can talk to and be sure of not getting silly answers and useless suggestions. Apparently I fix my gaze somewhere in his head behind his eyes and he is sure I am reading his thoughts. I'm not, though he is rather transparent and predictable. I'd say I can read him like a book but I can't read books so let's just use his favourite word, rapport. He and I have got it. A bit like the chap who strolls me round the grounds when he is tired of the classroom and can see that I am too.

I like those moments when company is easy, no demands. That's my main gripe about school. Almost all the time I'm there they're trying to get me to do things I'm not very good at. It's exhausting.

Every time I make it and complete one of their tasks, they up the stakes and think of ever greater complexity.

My skills inventory makes pretty depressing reading to the ignorant. My teacher got hold of our Lilli Nielsen functional and instructional schedule only to find I couldn't do any of the tasks in one of the sections, so she copied Trudy's idea which my mum uses at home and added other tasks that I *could* do and drew boxes for the ticks I would not otherwise have had. She wasn't cheating. We had told her the inventor of the schedule suggested she should do it because no one can anticipate every child's starting point and my achievements needed to be recorded and celebrated. Sounds OK to me.

Teamwork and joined-up thinking always surprise and impress me. It cheered my teacher up too.

In a nutshell
- The world beyond reach can be a mystery when the distance senses of sight or sound are missing.
- Take any movement as potentially communicative.
- Tiny achievements add up to great ones. Some people love recording these incremental steps.

Episode 4

A SENSE OF OTHERS

There was never a time when I didn't know the approximate shape of other people. I think it is because I always used to bath with my sister and she was in touch with me for large parts of our free time. Maybe it was because my uncle decided I shouldn't spend much time in prams and other baby containers. He'd been reading about stone-age cultures and thought I'd be better off as an Amerindian child forever astride someone's hip. As a result I had a pretty good idea of hips and arms and mouths and hands and all the other bits I came into regular contact with.

> Jean Liedloff in her book *The Continuum Concept* (1975: 64) describes Amazonian Indians carrying their children and considers the consequences for western children distanced from their carers by the use of buggies, cots, play pens and prams. A blind child in a pram can seem remote and even a sighted child has only the poor substitute of eye contact for the reassuring physical contact which Liedloff argues is essential for emotional development.
>
> Bowlby's early study (1951) and Harlow and Harlow's distressed apes in Foss (1961) also illustrate this argument cogently.

As I had never done the sort of foot research that typically developing babies do when they idly fiddle with their toes and bite them while lying on their backs, I had an incomplete body image as far as my own legs and feet were concerned and so I didn't realize the necessity to find out about other people's. My research project began when I was being shown off to a fellow who was some kind of disability roadshow. He had been summoned to sort out some of the dilemmas my nursery nurse was struggling with. I remember being surprised at his feet. Maybe it was the size as well as their existence that surprised me. Alice had been showing how much better my arm movements were if I was propped up in a sort of lotus position. The knot of my legs formed a lump for me to lean against. Alice had pulled off one of my socks and was telling the other people around that I seemed to prefer bare feet.

Everyone in the group had removed their shoes at the bottom of the nursery stairs (house rule) and someone had been playing footsy with my toes. I realized it was the chap who had come to advise us. He said I had very little information flowing in and I needed every channel I could get to receive information about the world and that bare feet were useful for finding out about all sorts of things. At that point he pulled his socks off and we were bare feet to bare feet. He pulled a tin tray over and put some chains in it so that I could create a racket. He and I poked and pulled the chains with our toes. Alice then showed him how our sand tray could be rested upside down on a couple of chairs to form an echoing roof over me while I played. Once the perspex dome was over me I found it very difficult to hear the conversation and so I concentrated on the tray, the chain and the enormous feet. I like having conversation muffled; it can be so distracting.

Gradually I found out that everyone has feet. They also have ankles and knees, but this discovery came later. Some of my school friends might as well not have these joints for all the use they are to them. My mum says mine aren't much good but they are handy when she's trying to manoeuvre me from my chair to the loo seat or onto a bed. Then I can be propped up on my legs while I turn and bend. They're also useful when I'm having a go on the standing frame and the chariot version that has huge wheels. Just as ear flaps are useful only for hooking glasses onto, so my legs are somewhere for the velcro straps to go and I end up as tall as people who can use their legs well.

An odd thing happens when I get strapped into tall gadgets. People start treating me differently. It must be something to do with babies being low down so people treat me like a baby when I'm low down. Upright, I get spoken to as if I have a brain and an opinion. (Since tiny children evidently have brains and opinions too this perhaps means that we ought to be treating them with more respect too.)

Linda Bidabe's MOVE curriculum began with the determination to get kids out of sitting into standing apparatus.

One of the things that happens when I'm low down is that people think I don't need to be consulted about where we are going, or kept informed as we travel about. But I do like to know. In fact it boils down to those four things that I need to know if I am to be fully functional. I need to know

- where I am
- who I'm with
- what's happening and
- what's happening next.

When people forget to keep me informed I get cross, frightened or I give up and withdraw. Can't be good. They are four of my top cravings, more than yoghurt and banana even. If I can't answer those questions, I'm not nice to be near. My teeth grind and I've been known to rip a foot strap from its mounting, such is the urgency of my enquiry.

Heather Murdoch suggested the fourth 'need to know' – what's happening next – when she was tutor in deafblind education at Birmingham University.

In a nutshell
- A blind child may not be aware of the whole picture but only the parts she has encountered.
- Challenging behaviour can mean there is some information the child has not had. Try answering the four questions and see if there is a change in that behaviour.

Episode 5

A SENSE OF ORDER

Perhaps my earliest memory is of that moment when I realized that I could predict what was happening. It's not that I was confused about events before that; it's just that the world seemed to me to be a place of random events over which I had no control – indeed, I think I hadn't any knowledge that it was a world over which there was any possibility of control. When it first sank in, I made a dramatic time-warp leap and came to understand more of my past. I pieced together some kind of formulation about events – another of those 'Aha!' moments when my head rang with that clunk that happens when a penny suddenly drops.

It all happened during a struggle at the doorway when my father was trying to get me and my sister and all the paraphernalia of childhood out to the car without letting the cat out. I kind of got the picture, a sense of what it was about, where we were going and who was involved. I couldn't tell you now which was the bit of information I got that set it all into an integrated whole but it was something about the farcical nature of my dad's panic and excitement which later turned out to be the birth of my brother.

All I knew was that we were visiting somewhere new and different for a definite purpose that my father had in mind. I think perhaps this might have been a key notion – the realization that Dad had a mind which he could have things in.

In the autism field people are familiar with the 'theory of mind' which is suggested as one of the pieces missing from the autistic person's make-up. They fail to see that others have a mind or that others are aware that they have a mind, so they make all sorts of misinterpretations – which Utta Frith has described. The part of the brain that processes this thinking can be observed in action through Positron Emissions Tomography or PET scans.

Blind children will also have trouble identifying other people's thoughts and reactions because they do not see the little shifts of expression or body, the nuances of behaviour by which sighted people communicate their internal states to each other – sometimes unwittingly. Those blind children who do not appreciate how other people think should not then be diagnosed as autistic as a consequence of their lateness in acquiring this 'theory of mind'. See Hobson (1993: 203–11).

So it was no surprise to me that I was unpacked from the car at a totally new location. It had a name I did not recognize, a ramp that rattled in a way no other ramp had rattled, a hissing doorway to a bleeping, humming and malodorous foyer.

I love 'malodorous'; it's one of my key categories for classifying smells. There are 71 malodours I am aware of so far; there are innumerable odours that leave me unmoved, but the scents I enjoy are pretty much limited to a dozen or so in number. This was a new one: malodour; subcategory: hospitals, administration and carpets, new, itchy.

They seemed to have got to my sister too. She nudged me and said 'phwar' and she knew I knew what she meant. We rattled along cavernous corridors with some very strange bumps and slopes. I recognized each of these the next day when we came to collect the new babe and Mum. My favourite was a loose inspection cover which turned out conveniently to be a yard short of Mum's room where we hung a right.

Training courses in rehabilitation and mobility train people to operate by this mapping system, identifying the sort of landmarks that a blind person would need in order to recognize and learn routes. Although this training does not normally focus on the needs of people in wheelchairs, the same need to know is present and the information transmitted through the vehicle or by its twists and turns and inclines can be processed and used to form an understanding or internal map.

The features on this hospital route are not the ones a sighted person would necessarily attend to and are examples of the way we each operate in different sensory worlds.

Mum's bed was high. I had to be lifted 'hup' onto it. Mum was hampered by stuff on the back of her hand which she didn't mention but it interfered with her ritual caressing of me. I was introduced to number two son and malodour 48 – soon to become a proper classifiable scent once I'd got used to him.

Odd how, after a while, smells leach into each other. They leave a sort of conglomerate tribal smell, the kind that tells you when you wake up where you are. It can be confusing when smells linger but the thing that made the smell has gone. It took me ages to cotton on to that, longer still to appreciate that smells can be made about things that never were there – like smoky bacon crisps that have never been near smoke or bacon. Strangest of all is the smell of smoky bacon crisps that comes from a machine that makes smells in our school sensory room; there aren't even any crisps, as far as I know.

Rosemary has a screaming fit every time that smells machine goes on. She can't stand crisps so she splutters and blows raspberries. Mary, her support worker, loves smoky bacon so we get it every time we go in and of course Rosemary gets in a state every time we go in. Mary thinks Rosemary is not very fond of the flashing lights. She'll work it out one day. We have to be very patient with teachers and their support staff. (That's not a universal truth.)

My mate Anthony is very impatient. He bites people when they make mistakes like that. He also bites people when they get things right, which makes communication tricky.

The sudden dawning of the nature of orderliness and sequencing of events came as I began to make connections and put my experiences into groups; manageable chunks. Not everything fits neatly into my scheme. After all, there are still many events which are neither orderly nor obviously in any sequence. It was when I started hanging on to markers of events that Mum started helping me collect things to do with our regular activities. Dad put a shelf up along the side of my bed with dozens of markers arranged along it. By markers I mean objects that had come to have particular significance for me.

It began when I got the paper bag under my arm – the bag that had had the stale bread in for the ducks. Mum had announced in the park as usual that the bread was all gone and made to take the bag from me and dispose of it. I squeezed my ribs against my biceps and the bag tore. I trumpeted triumphantly. Mum prized it out of my grasp and stepped to the litter bin at the lake side. I grizzled and did my famous Depression routine. At the third or fourth attempt over the next weeks, she eventually relented and let me keep the bag which I managed to hang on to until bedtime. Next morning when I mentioned it by squeezing my ribs against my biceps like a thing demented, she got the bag out of my bin and decided to let me keep it.

Just as I had appreciated that my dad could have things in mind, so she had discovered that I had things in my mind too and could indicate what this was by gesture and mime. She saw my action and read my mind.

According to a visitor at school, we had invented 'objects of reference' but I think of it as *the paper bag connection*. Nowadays I have 11 bags which all have different functions and when Mum gives me one of them I know which of the 11 jobs we are about to undertake. Most of the bags are not paper, which is my favourite material, but they are all important in my campaign to understand which of all the things I do is the one we are going to do next.

> Objects of reference were first pioneered as a structured communication system in Holland for deafblind people and the name is an unedifying translation. Keith Park and Adam Ockelford in the UK have published some useful books and articles on how they can be introduced and extended. They are very significant for people who have hearing as well as visual difficulties and are gaining popularity with clients in all sorts of settings for whom spoken or signed language is problematic conceptually. Ockelford's third edition of *Objects of Reference* (2000) is now available from the RNIB.

One of my teachers did a course on communication with objects and Rosemary had a trayful of signifier bits which she rummaged through as the collection grew. I remember one occasion when she demonstrated how she had failed to get the point. She had been given a little string of bells as her signifier of 'we're off for a music session with Jim in the hall'. She merrily jangled her bells but as we approached the hall she heard the dreaded sound of Jim's accordion and expressed in a variety of dangerous ways how she hated these mock folk dance sessions. It was clear to our teacher that the jingle bells strategy had not worked. She did not associate them with the activity therefore they were not fulfilling their role as communication aids. The classroom team discussed this and decided to identify something in the folk dance activity that Rosemary could take away with her from the hall so that she would have an object that *she* associated with the activity. They gave her a little toy accordion that was so ghastly it must have been free in a cracker. She played it as a kind of cacophonous counter-melody during our dancing and, true enough, next time we were readying ourselves for dance again, she was presented with the toy and she had her outburst in the classroom instead of near the hall. It had worked. She could remember and simultaneously anticipate what it was she disliked. After a few moments she calmed down, having plucked up the courage to face the awful lesson and having been convinced that immediately following it there would be peanut treats and a drink. The treats and drink were in her object tray in the partition next along from the accordion. We took the symbols for peanuts and drink with us to the hall so that they were on hand at the end of the session to get her motivated to return to class. Nowadays she just has a little weep or sigh when she holds the accordion. Once I got it under an elbow and managed to squeeze it. It was strangely satisfying to hear her whimper in the corner but a tribute to the power of objects of reference.

The thing I liked most about knowing my own timetable in the early days was that it allowed me to relax on nursery days when I knew the routine. There are times when I think of routine as being the same as boredom but normally I settle for knowing what's going on in a familiar sequence rather than confusion and disorder. These are just two of the things which get me agitated. On balance I'd rather have the certainty of clockwork ritual. The occasional excitement of the unexpected can then be enjoyed without anxiety and stress.

It was a long time before I could relax at weekends and on holidays. We had a consultant once who was going to put me on a muscle relaxant because of my tension but my aunt said she thought I used my spastic tensions to communicate with and if that was numbed, how could I express myself? They numbed me anyhow and it brought certain other advantages which probably outweigh what was lost – there are always other ways to communicate and my aunt and I have been researching some alternatives.

On my days with her, known as 'giving Mum a break', we sit face-to-face. My aunt calls it 'sitting face-to-face' so that must be what we do.

I'm not very good at faces. People sometimes show me their faces, drawing my attention to some of their features – especially men with beards like my uncle. They don't seem to realize that this is only important when they are actually up against me. Once they are away, which is most of the time, I can't use the fact that they have whatever it is. These seem to matter to them in a way that I may one day study, if I have the time.

I can hear beards and moustaches. Men always seem to be scratching them, stroking them, sucking them and filtering their speech through them so I know what they sound like all the time they are speaking or agitated and itchy. What beards feel like is less interesting to me than they think.

For some obscure reason, my aunt wants me to be a face-to-face sort of person. She's been beavering away at it for years. In fact, I think we get on best when she sits me between her knees with us both facing the same way. She nuzzles my neck and speaks right into my ear. I think this is preferable to being spat at and breathed into – especially when someone I don't know very well is showing me how something works. If they embrace me from behind and I can feel what their arms are doing, I get a much better impression of their activity.

Face-to-face interaction is so fundamental to human communi-cation from day one that it is hard for sighted people to conceive of a life without it. Newborn babies are equipped with ready responses to faces. Daniel Stern and Colwyn Trevarthen have written extensively on research in this area. Stroke and other head injury victims can lose this ability to read and recognize faces. The capacity can be absent or dysfunctional in children whose brains have developed abnormally. In such cases it can be fruitless trying to teach these skills if the organ for their retention is missing.

Most people seem to think I want them opposite me; they take my hands and show me the movements. It occurred to me that in this position they are clumsier as they are doing the task the wrong way round. This is most obvious when they help me eat. Their familiar movements are reversed, spooning food away from themselves with the wrong hand. This is usually accomplished with a barrage of words about the food, the weather or the TV which always distracts me from the puzzling process of getting stuff down my throat.

It still surprises me when my swallow reflex hits a suitable moment in my breathing cycle and the food slithers down without choking me. Lord knows how many bits of old dinner are languishing in my lungs. Perhaps if people would stand behind me and share arm and hand in the scooping, lifting and shovelling, staying silent so I could concentrate on the job in hand, then I'd be a more successful eater.

We had a music lesson once when our teacher decided not to talk. She brought the trolley in with great rattlings and bangings as usual, dished out the percussion, hammered away on the piano as usual, cleared up and trundled the trolley out and as she did so Rosemary said 'More.' It was her first word and it happened in the session when the teacher didn't speak. Miraculous.

A group of Canadian researchers (Biederman *et al.* 1994) showed that children learn a task more quickly if you stop talking to them about it. The children in the research had problems unravelling speech and had to stop what they were doing to listen. Speech can become an obstacle.

Anthony made such a pig's ear of swallowing he has ended up with a gadget on his belly through which the school nurse, and presumably his mum, pump nutrients.

I said 'presumably his mum' because I have never been to his house to find out. Funny how my best friend and I don't get together after school. My sister always seems to have people round and they have become friends of mine now, but it's not like having your own friends round, I imagine. That can be my next project, to grab Anthony between my biceps and ribs and bring him to add to my collection on the shelf above my bed! Can't imagine that would go down well with Anthony's escort. How would we get him in my cab? It's already full of my wheelchair and standing frame. I'd be willing to swap a night's standing frame homework for Anthony's company at tea. Sounds a fair deal to me. I'll work on it.

I think it unlikely I'll be invited to stay the night, though it is not unthinkable. I sometimes stay at my aunt's. There has always been an agreement that if Mum and Dad were both ill, we three could all go there but my uncle thought it would be a good idea to have a dummy run with me as I am the most complicated. They also planned to have the baby and my sister so that my parents could concentrate on me for a bit. I am rarely their full-time job at any one time and it would be nice to have their undivided attention for a while.

Trudy says I should go for short breaks to a special centre for kids like me but my mum says she didn't have kids just to parcel them off to strangers. It's hard for me to see things from any point of view different from my mum's. It would seem disloyal. She is such a formative influence on me. Nevertheless there are occasions when I see things differently from her – that is not to say that I think she is wrong, just that there is more than one way of seeing things. (Since I can't see, my point of view is going to be hard to get in touch with – if I can be said to have 'a point of view' at all.) I do have an independent opinion. I would like to try one of these respite places my social worker always mentions on her visits.

Rosemary goes once a fortnight for a weekend's respite care and has different transport and escorts to take her straight from school on a Friday, returning her the next Monday morning. Her parents get virtually four days off. Mind you, if I lived with Rosemary I'd want regular breaks too. She can be pretty relentless when she gets into her nothing's-good-enough rut. My teacher sends her out to the soft play area with a helper all to herself. Perhaps I should try being impossible and see if I can't get an extra dose of soft play. I'd really only want to go there to get away from Rosemary when she is being impossible and since that is the time she goes, I think she is always going to get ahead of me and more than her share. Such is life.

When Dave Wood was deputy head at RNIB Rushton Hall School he introduced a policy that no children should be taken to recreational facilities for withdrawal as a consequence of their unacceptable behaviour. Children who resist group work may learn to manipulate staff into giving them 'Time Out'. The argument is that such pleasurable activities need to be timetabled so that children know they visit them on schedule rather than on demand; these fine environments might become associated with disturbed behaviour rather than enjoyment and learning.

In a nutshell
- A clearly defined sequence of events may help disruptive as well as withdrawn children to understand what is expected of them and enable them to participate more fully.
- The world is full of landmarks that help us know where we are. Some people may need help in identifying these systematically.
- Movements are clues about what is happening but smells can linger from things that are no longer there and be confusing.
- An object from an activity can be presented once the person knows that it is part of an activity. It can then come to stand for that activity in the person's mind, much as words do. It then becomes the means to anticipate that event. First introduction of the object out of the context of the activity could usefully be presented after the time of its use at the end of a day when we reminisce about what has happened.
- Watch for actions that let us know the person is experiencing pleasure or displeasure and react to these as if they were a communication.
- Try working around a blind child from behind and see if they respond differently. Find out which they prefer or which side they like to be approached from.

- Persevere with stuctured routines so that children can become familiar with them and later discover how inevitably they vary and that change can be endured.
- Words are the sort of thing that help people who are helped by that sort of thing.

Episode 6

A SENSE OF SPACE

When we first worked on the idea of spending time in tiny spaces, I began to enjoy fumbling with things that hung around me. At first I didn't find the choice of playthings very enthralling and my mum thought the idea wasn't working. Then Trudy and Gran went on a course and came back with missionary zeal to hang things around me that were really important and interesting. I was amazed to find knives and forks and spoons dangling around me as well as all my feeding and toileting paraphernalia. I had never got my hands on a nappy before and was amazed to find the sticky tabs and things that I had sort of known about because of people wrapping them around my midriff but it isn't the same as actually having time to study them in peace.

I do best by gently stroking things with the back of my hand. This action usually knocks things away from me and is very frustrating as I still cannot use my available vision to locate things like that. My dad used to complain about the platform and the little room I worked in. We only had a small house (without the extension at first) and it seemed to take up a lot of space. My sister painted the platform in what my aunt called her after-Picasso style – whatever that means. From then on it hung on nails on the kitchen wall and was a famous work of art in our street as it could be seen by passers-by who were dead impressed. My dad said I should be shoved in the cupboard under the stairs. Trudy thought that was a brilliant idea but my mum needed the space for Hoovers and things. Dad and Trudy applied for a grant and got a garden shed paid for. All the clutter from the hole under the stairs went in there and I got a splendid place to yell and fidget in. The acoustics in there are brilliant.

For a change sometimes, I go in the empty bath with a clothes drier over me from which a different assortment of things dangles. In some ways I prefer this to the cupboard under the stairs. If I decide to play with loose things they cannot roll away from me and I can always feel where they have rolled to. Once I managed to break all the strings holding my objects so everything was clonking about in the bottom of the bath with me as I wriggled. This struck me as quite amusing but my dad called me a wrecker and fixed things back on with tough elastic. Trudy said I was more interested in the elastic and how my dad had fixed it than the things attached when she saw me feeling the bars of the clothes drier. She said it showed how intelligent I was. Unfortunately none of the educational psychologists test me on this particular skill when they come to measure my progress or lack of it.

They don't see me at my best. I think I'm most fully functional in the bath and remember another of those occasions I'd like to recreate but can't – time to play in a bath with no water in it, just a few of my favourite things. It was in the bath that I first realized that the things I knock away still exist; the water held them close to me on a single plain of floating and the things that sink were all against me. I managed to search the whole bath to find the things I had lost.

> Children with complex disabilities who do not use their sight are late to develop what Piaget described as object constancy, especially those objects that make no noise. How are they to know these things still exist out there?

There's one chap who came and wanted to know if I knew any nursery rhymes. Because I couldn't recite or sing any he decided I didn't know any – which is not the same thing. This was at a time when I was really into Ted Hughes and regarded my baby brother's choice of tapes as terribly immature.

> **In a nutshell**
> - Play can be supported by enclosing the disabled child in a small space and attaching interesting articles all around.

Episode 7

A SENSE OF BELONGING

Trudy came round one day when Mum had got a grant to adapt a back room into a shower and changing room for me. They were discussing layout and decor. Apparently they'd decided I was going to have the wall around my window white and the opposite one navy blue. Trudy reckoned I'd be able to tell which way round I was facing because of the light and dark opposite each other. Hadn't they got this topsy turvy? If I had been involved I think I would have had dark paint on the window wall as that is the dark end and white paint on the wall where the daylight shines. I'm going to end up with the dark bit lightened and the light bit darkened and it'll all end up lukewarm. We'll see, perhaps Trudy's right. She usually is.

I relaxed through their discussion; it's no big deal as I already know which way I'm facing and I won't really mind what colour they paint the walls. The echoes from the window wall are unlike any other echoes and change drastically with the drawing of the curtains. There's a double clue really because the echoes from the wall and the window are different and the curtains don't echo but there's also the effect of the windows being different at night from in the daytime. I know my sighted friends and family attach huge importance to this difference in sunlight or dark but it hasn't been much help to me for some reason. I'm more interested in how cold windows are at night and how warm on a sunny day. I can feel the heat or the cold from across the room – just as I can feel the heat of people's bodies from quite a distance. It's nice being able to have cuddles across space when it's someone you like. Strangers are just as warm but their warmth isn't like cuddles.

My talking thermometer can register big differences in temperature but doesn't seem to attach much importance to some of the warmths

I can notice changing – especially those which drift across my face on the stirring of the air. I don't think my thermometer is quick enough to announce changes that are so fleeting. But then a thermometer doesn't need to know where people are and where they're moving to. The thermometer just says how warm it is rather than where the warmth is coming from. I think where it comes from is more important than how hot it actually is. If I couldn't feel the warmth of a person approaching I'm sure I'd jump out of my skin whenever a stealthy person crept up on me without warning.

I got a bit tense when I learned that in my bedroom I'm going to have warm air ducts. This is going to take some getting used to. I suspect it is going to be like most improvements – it will have its down side. Lets hope there won't be a noisy fan whirring away and shutting out things I need to hear. I'm going to have to rely on other means of gauging where people are. There are going to be all sorts of warm currents of air that don't mean anything. I don't mind this out of doors but I've come to rely on these little draughts indoors as explanations for what is going on. Of course outdoor currents of air are not entirely meaningless. They bring messages of smell. These are usually too general to be useful but I can tell about the weather, especially recent rain, and what is blooming with the seasonal changes. My favourite is rape; the air has a sort of chewable texture and my dad's hay fever makes him sound all gruff and hostile. He doesn't think it's funny when I chuckle at his misfortune.

I managed to get my mum to buy rapeseed oil in Tesco last week. I got hold of a display stand and gripped my teeth at her when she read out the name on the label. Recently she has been noticing this grimace of mine and has started responding to me as if I were telling her something. This is Trudy's latest campaign. She leaves my mum with homework each week and comes to find out what success we've been having at guessing the meaning of the grimace. Trudy says I probably don't mean anything by the gritting of my teeth but people should react as if I were meaning something then I can use the grimace in order to tell people things or ask for things. What Trudy doesn't know is that I've been doing this off and on for ages but had given up because nobody seemed to notice.

I've found that if I combine the bite with a grunt and a flailing of arms then people often do think of what I might be saying if I could. I think the rapeseed oil is the first proper victory. I had an egg fried in it tonight. It definitely tastes different. My dad had one too but unfortunately he didn't go all husky and when I laughed he thought I was enjoying the egg. Apparently a bit of egg flew onto his plate when I laughed and he picked it out and returned it. I wouldn't have minded if he'd eaten it – one bit of egg is much like any other.

I was sitting on Dad's knee once at some sort of assessment meeting where he was absent-mindedly jogging up and down. He was sounding all sad and telling a David Brown person that he wished he could communicate with his son – he meant me. He stopped jiggling so I bounced myself up and down. He said 'Sorry, I didn't mean to stop', and carried on entertaining me with his knees. Mr Brown pointed out that this was perfectly valid communication. I had told him what stimulus I wanted and Dad had provided it. It changed our family's definition of communication and they stopped saying I couldn't do it – it was just that I couldn't say the words.

It may be that up to 80 per cent of what is meant is conveyed non-verbally in normal discourse. Try saying out loud 'The boy rode his bike to the shop' and put the stress on the word boy. You are telling the listener that it isn't the girl. If you stress 'rode' then your listener understands that he didn't push it. If you stress 'to', then you know that it wasn't from and if you emphasize 'shop', we know it wasn't, for example, the cinema. This dynamic quality of speech is confirmed or contradicted by body movements, facial expressions, gesture, volume and speed, all aspects of the communication that carry meaning and which tiny babies observe and monitor long before the words convey much at all (see Gopnik *et al.* 2000).

Mum spoke at a conference a few weeks ago. It sounded weird with her voice amplified and coming from several places at once. I couldn't tell where she was. She and Trudy had planned what to say and Mum had practised it at home twice to check the timing, so I know it word for word. She sounded terrified on the big occasion; I hadn't heard her like that before. She must have noticed too because she said she would never do it again. That's a shame, because we had an all-expenses-paid trip to somewhere we'd never been before and I enjoyed the adventure.

Mum said that everyone looking after a child like me should have a secretary and chauffeur in addition to the room extension she'd already got. People laughed but I think she meant it. She told other home visitors like Trudy that they should tread gently – 'Treading Gently' was the title of her talk. She told her audience that her new extension has a wider door than usual, even for disabled access, to allow for the throng of visitors. She wished she had had one of those water boilers installed too since these professionals always seem to want tea or coffee; that way they could make their own. She added that tea and coffee should also be provided by the state along with the chauffeur and secretary.

She described Trudy's hands-off approach to us. She hardly ever held or touched me, never supported my eating or took me off to do magical expert rituals with me. She just talked to Mum about ways of doing things so that it was Mum and the family who got to be deft in handling my peculiarities. Trudy once told Mum that it was not her business to show how good she was at managing my disabilities – she only pops in once in a while; the skill needed to be within the home. It wasn't long into our relationship that Trudy only came on days when my uncle could make it too as he had made me into a bit of a project to keep himself out of mischief while unemployed. It was Trudy who said she trod lightly when stepping into our web of relationships. My dad said he was in the same boat; he used to hover around the edge of me and Mum for years until my uncle sent them off on a dirty weekend so they could try spending time with each other instead of always with me. Dad came back with a definite role; while Mum was holding me near the TV, he would massage her scalp and occasionally mine too. It definitely made a difference and his treading into the Mum-and-me zone was very light.

> Daniel N. Stern recommends this gentle approach in his book *The Motherhood Constellation* (1995).

Mum told her audience she was thinking of applying to the *Guinness Book of Records* for having the most medical appointments to attend in a year as I was under so many specialists. She asked them not to condemn her for turning down some of the appointments as she had developed a strategy: after one visit, if any specialist asked her more than they told her, and called her the expert on me, then she didn't bother going again. It's not that she's against research; it's just that time and distance turn all these meetings into whole-day events – and sometimes overnight stays – and she is not paid to be a research assistant. However, if the visit makes a difference to my well-being, then she troops along to get some more of the information we need.

She complained that the sanctuary of her home suddenly became a public place into which a stream of new workers marched. She described how she was stressed, distressed and depressed. (She made it sound quite poetic.) She was in no state to take on board all their new jargon or to make allowances for their individual foibles. She apologized for her unrelenting ingratitude; after all, she didn't want my disabilities so why should she welcome those who came to attend to them? I think the listeners expected her to sound bitter but she was referring to a sort of running gag that she and Trudy tossed about in their banter. Mum promised to be grateful when Trudy came up with 17 cures for my 17 conditions. It was all part of my barometer for telling how they were getting on.

The day they really established rapport was when they both cried. Trudy had been coasting along on her tide of charisma, specialist know-how and charm and was running out of steam, I thought. After the crying they seemed to forge a new partnership and could rage a little more without falling out. Mum got more enthusiastic about the ideas Trudy and she discussed and I could tell she was actually carrying out all the suggestions, modifying them and reporting back systematically. She now has several thick note pads of all the things that she and Trudy get up to with me. This frightens the socks off some of the specialists we see because Mum gives them a good grilling and is getting an amazing vocabulary of medical terms.

My hunch is that my relationship with my mum has hotted up in parallel with her relationship with Trudy. She has become more interested in me as a person and sees me less as a complicated set of chores to be done. I can feel my isolation dissolve the more we get enmeshed. The way she deals with me is evolving and changing. It is quite unlike the way she is with the baby. That all seems to be spontaneous and natural, more like her mother was with her, she says. They don't have much expert intervention. They manage their choreographed duet relatively effortlessly and call to each other in an elegant dialogue through space and turmoil. There is no Trudy to facilitate this psychological pair.

Bowlby examines this process in detail in his publications on attachment, and Anne Alvarez in her book *Live Company* (1992) says there is no such thing as an individual psychology, only the psychology of pairs. Colwyn Trevarthen has published reams on mother–baby micro-analysis of interaction (1979).

I register these differences and regret the periods when we only engage with the chores and routines of a demanding domestic schedule and miss the chances to get to grips with each other. I think that is why my uncle is so good for me; he spends time with me when all the chores are done and it is his choice to make our lives richer in a calculated sort of way, planned and executed so as to be exhilarating. He wouldn't see it this way as he is such a spontaneous sort of loony, but he has organized things so that there is time and place in which to be effectively loony and spontaneous.

He has some coarse expressions my mum would not approve of; when we are off the scale on some frenzied activity he screams abuse at the curriculum and challenges my teachers to find a box to tick that in. We spent a hilarious hour once filling in the same sort of checklist that my teacher had been creative with. If you stick to the list you can get depressed about all the things I can't do. It came on the same day as we read Douglas Adams' and John Lloyd's ridiculous book, *The Meaning of Liff*, and we discovered we could fart in harmony. There was no category for this skill area so one had to be added. It was during this or a similar encounter that I remembered my discovery of feet. I had tended to be aware of differences more than similarities. I added to a catalogue in my head which lists samenesses. It was another of those days when I learned more about other people's bodies. I had had my feet massaged and then my uncle took his socks off, put his feet on my lap and told me to do his.

That role reversal caused a shift in my thinking; call it cognitive dissonance if you will. It was one of those moments when the world does not fit your preconception and you have to reorganize your thinking, a bit like that jarring sensation I get when someone carries me up stairs, thinks there is one more step when there isn't and nearly collapses in a heap. My dad always counts the steps out loud to stop him doing this. He doesn't do it when he is on his own mounting the stairs and I reckon that must have to do with him not being able to see stairs when he's carrying me. Yes, that must be it. Recently, with me getting bigger, he has been carrying me on his back and he doesn't have to count any more.

I love being carried on backs. I get such a clear impression of who I am with, what they are doing and where we are going. Voices, especially men's (who are usually the ones who piggyback me) feel wonderful there. I have a cousin who is a heavy smoker and the smell of him and the sound of his cough are awe-inspiring when he carries me. Once he even managed to smoke while he did it – until my mum dared him ever to do it again! I rather liked it, though I usually find tobacco smoke irritating. Trudy thinks mints disguise the smell of her tobacco but mints on their own smell quite different from mints and tobacco combined. There is no disguising smells.

This cousin read me a passage from *Under the Eye of the Clock* in which Christy Nolan is taken behind the bike sheds of his mainstream school by a gang of smokers and has his lips clamped around a fag and his nose pinched so he has to inhale. Not exactly core curriculum stuff, but definitely a key learning experience. Life is sometimes interminably dull when there aren't enough of these moments to satisfy my hunger for events.

In a nutshell
- There are clues in the environment which help us orient ourselves. Emphasizing these is not always necessary for a blind person who already uses features of which sighted people may not be aware.
- A special bond exists between the primary care giver and the child which is strongest when that is also the mother; this process can be interrupted by disability.

A SENSE OF OCCASION

In the early days, Trudy and my mum used to read articles to find ideas for things to do with me and strategies to try. Trudy was sent into the garden one time to find a riddle – one of those big sieves you sift the soil with. She came back with this huge rusty thing which the article said they should balance on my chest. An assortment of balls was put in it and as I breathed in and out the balls rolled to and fro. The idea was to see if I could become aware of the movement of the ball being something to do with the movement of my ribs as my lungs expanded and contracted.

They started swapping balls and trying single ones to see if any turned me on. I found them pretty well uniformly dull until there was only a cotton doll's-head ball which rolled oh so gently and made the littlest of sounds. It was like auto-tickling and got me giggling. This also got me spluttering and choking, at which point the riddle fell off and clattered around on the resonating platform which I was lying on at the time. Fortunately my sister spotted my involvement in the microseconds before I choked, so I was given another go after I had revived my normal breathing pattern. Trudy got very excited and said she had proved that I could make connections between cause and effect, so they filled in a form about functional dependency. Apparently I had twigged that the rolling of the feather-light ball depended on my chest movements and I changed the rate of my breathing to bring variation to the rolling. There ensued a debate about whether this was indeed functional dependency, cause and effect, or should they call it intentionality?

The next time we went to the Sense family centre in Ealing, they confirmed that it was all three. They said they didn't care what we called it so long as we recognized my achievement in noticing what

I had done and that I could produce change in my immediate environment. Trudy and Mum were both cheered up at this confirmation but I had forebodings. It occurred to me that if this news got about, all and sundry would be raising their expectations and demanding that I do this sort of thing all day, every day.

My sister told me of a similar experience she had when she read book 3b of a reading scheme her teacher liked to use. She had noticed there were 28 in the series and a, b, c and d at each of those levels. Neither of us could count to 112 at the time but we both were aghast at the prospect of a yard-long project of densely worded pages. There was no such shelf full for me to contemplate so, for all I knew at the time, my teacher might produce an endless stream of examples of functions for me to find prompts they depended on. Switches in our soft room were a case in point. We had a computerized program that changed the way the lights and sounds responded to the operation of the switches. No sooner had I grasped the fact that I had to raise my arm to make the light come on than the computer decided I had to wave it twice or further or higher to get the same result. It also printed out incontrovertible proof of how hard I had worked so that everyone would know if I was slacking next time. I had my off days when I had the intention but not the wherewithal to exceed my previous attainment level. Trudy told my teacher to see whether other factors were at work: how long was it since my last dose of epilim, how long since my last meal or drink? There was no printout from the computer about whether I was feeling bloody-minded or not, though on some occasions it must have been pretty obvious that I was simply unwilling to play the game. Computers can be dim.

I have a vague memory of something Trudy tried out on an early visit on an occasion when she had decided I was depressed. She had been unable to interest me in anything at all and had hung a paper tissue just in front of my mouth so that as I breathed in it touched my lips and as I breathed out it drifted away. She tried tissue paper and tin foil as well as streamers from a party popper. I remember quite liking the smell of explosives from the party popper on the paper and twitching my nose and lips in response. They were discussing ways of getting me interested in seven different air stream items so that I could associate each with a day of the week. I had some cotton wool with bleach in it for chlorine-scented swimming days, a little bundle of straw for the day I went riding. I can't remember the others as my mum lost interest in it before I had learned what all seven were for. Events caught up with us – oversleeping days, hospital appointment days and the like and the routine was lost so that now I can only recall fragments. Since I am now very confident about which day of the week it always is, perhaps my mum abandoned it once I had got the point of the cyclical nature of days and their associated activities.

It's easier to lose track of the days in extended holiday times when days could be much like one another. My grandmother was more routine-oriented than Mum; she would hoover behind certain furniture on certain days and change bed linen and launder, iron and dust at the same time on the same day each week. Mum is more chaotic and laundry seems to be a daily thing and shopping expeditions more crisis management than planning around a menu like grandma's was. Her shopping depended on when opening times used to be, so she would never dream of going to Tesco at night – though my dad and I often do, just to escape the crowds. We have to get there before eight if we need the pharmacy department and it means the cafe isn't open too, and I miss that little ritual. Usually we get a kebab from a van to compensate and I have to promise not to tell Mum. I always keep my promise but when she tucks me in to bed she says something along the lines of 'Phwoar, you've been to that kebab place again, I can smell the fumes from here'. It is amazing how much my mum gets without me having to speak, which is just as well since speaking is still one of the things I feel I never will accomplish. This doesn't often get me down, though there are occasions when I think of something witty to contribute to a classroom or family conversation.

I suppose that's one of the things I like about my uncle – he chatters away inanely but entertainingly and speaks as if I would appreciate his sense of humour. He often announces what he thinks I'm thinking and what my preferences would be if I could articulate them. On the occasions when he is right it is a kind of bull's-eye transaction and worth the dozen missed hits.

> The bull's-eye transaction is an expression of Eric Berne's and refers to an intimate event that reaches deep into the person, beyond egostates; see Berne (1973).

This must be what it is like to make autonomous choices, getting what you want and need at the time it is wished for. I remember one rather trivial example at a wedding when a cousin was trying to get champagne down me and our joint uncle arrived with my Tommy Tippee mug with a nozzle on top so that I could enjoy it properly without wasting any. Fortunately it was the one he had sprayed gold some weeks before because he thought it looked too infantile for a big lad like me and he had tied some silver ribbon round it for the occasion. It was the elasticated kind and he and I had worked out a way of getting my fingers wedged in it so I was holding it while he operated my elbow. He kept shoving my arm up in the air and shouting 'cheers m'dears'. I don't think I would have done that bit had I been doing it on my own but it was in tune with the festive spirit (or sparkling wine).

In a nutshell
- Tiny events can be very significant in discovering what a person understands or experiences.
- Small adaptations can make objects and activities age-appropriate as well as need-appropriate.

Episode 9

A SENSE OF CONTROL

There are times when I feel bodiless; I seem to float as a muddle of memories without sensation. This is bearable for a few minutes. It can also be a place for me to escape to deliberately. When I want to renew my contact with the world I only have to rock and I have a stream of sensations that tell me immediately what I am sitting or lying on and which way up I am. I survived a behaviour modification programme to eliminate my rocking behaviour some years ago. Fortunately Trudy managed to stop the procedure when she convinced the school that we didn't mind the bald spot at the back of my head and that I needed to be able to rock as a comfort, an information-seeking method and a form of protest. Most people I know now try to find out what I am doing my rocking for.

A. H. Estevis and A. J. Koenig (1994) report on such an intervention in the journal *Re:view 26*. The next issue contains a letter from Robert Orr and Suzie Potter urging rockers to rock on. The article by Elaine McHugh and Jean Pyfer (1999) reveals the complexity of this issue.

Anthony has a blood-curdling scream which he produces in delicate situations. Our mobility man was asked to help put a stop to this but he insisted he was there to get children to do more, not less, so he cogitated and came up with a theory that Anthony was exploring large spaces with his voice – churches for example. Screams in church are very exhilarating. He taught Anthony to clap which also produced a nice echo but was rather more socially acceptable. I click my tongue or listen to the echoes from my squeaky wheel when I want to know how big a strange place is. It's a useful source of information when entering a hall. You can tell whether it is empty or not by the way sounds reverberate.

If I sit quite still I soon drift away. Most people I know can sit as quietly as a mouse but still somehow manage to follow everything that is going on. I think this is maybe to do with the fact that they can see and this means they can know what is going on without actually seeming to do anything at all. I worked out recently that they can even see things that are not moving and are not making any sound at all. This would be a marvellous thing to be able to do. Things really only exist for me when they are noisily active, smell distinctive or give off heat.

Sometimes people offer me things that seem sensationless. I can tell when I have one of these vague things by me because they stop some movement or other. I bump against them and discover they are there. My sister thinks my favourite toy is a huge ball and she brings it to me whenever she is bored, thinking that it will solve my boredom problem too. She gets quite excited about it, chasing about all over the place. When it is my turn to hold it I let it go and squeal as it rolls away; I have to act for her sake. In fact the particular ball I am thinking of is hardly there at all. It has almost no weight and makes hardly any sound. I only know it is a ball because that is what my sister calls it. For a long time I could not understand why I could not get my hands to meet in the middle and eventually worked out that it was because Sis had put that weightless ball on my lap.

In some ways it reminds me of our school physio ball which I remember working out must be a sphere like other balls but is so big that I will never be able to get my arms around it however big I grow. In fact I prefer a real, ancient, leather football with the record of its triumphs and disasters ingrained in its textures, though my favourite ball is one of my mum's squash balls. It is split and so she doesn't want it back. I like it because it reminds me of the days we play in the squash court.

The local leisure centre lets us rent a court very cheaply on quiet days and we have invented all sorts of games. The one I really hate is when she grabs me by the ankles and swishes me across the floor until I crash into the metal plate – the one which players have to serve above in the proper game. I've tried becoming hysterical but that doesn't stop her. At the other end is a door that crashes when I slide into it. Everywhere else in the room is solid wall and provides the most wonderful echoes. Sometimes my sister comes too and gallops around yelling instructions to me that I can't obey and asking questions that I can't answer. But I can hear exactly where she is and so I can make balls roll towards her – or away from her if I am feeling uncooperative.

Once I managed to cling on to my crocodile in the morning and got my mum to bring it with us. You pull the string and it rattles a bit then shoots off, powered by little paddles on its legs. We managed to work out a way of me winding it up by Mum holding the string and me yanking the crocodile away from her with a two-handed grip I have developed which seems to involve my wrists more than my hands (which don't work very well). Once I got a round of applause from some squash players in the gallery when I accidentally kicked the crocodile and sent it flying into the metal plate end.

We play a marble game too. Once I played this game with a foreign visitor who watched me roll over some marbles and get one in my mouth. My mum gasped and rushed to me to fish it out. The visitor shouted 'Do not interfere! I have not lost a child yet.' and gave me a long lecture on the problems of spastic tongues and jaws and how to get things out from behind your teeth. This was all very well but I had a marble stuck in my mouth and I found it hard to concentrate on the finer points of mouth motor function (which she kept calling it). When I opened my mouth wide and the marble fell out my mother, who had been holding her breath, sighed with relief. A few moments later I came across another marble – could have been the same one – got it in my mouth and showed it gleefully to my mum.

I spat it out provocatively in her direction. Our visitor announced that I had now mastered this function which I would have been prevented from learning if Mother had rescued me.

This incident may be familiar to people who attended a lecture and workshop in Worthing on Active Learning where Lilli Nielsen demonstrated her innovative techniques. She sets up a play space which challenges the level of passivity blind children can lapse into and allows them to discover for themselves the extent to which they can become the one to cause events. Her book *Space and Self* (1992) explains much of this approach. It is available from the RNIB.

Mum bought me some little indoor golf balls, like table tennis balls with holes in, so that I could practise this 'mouth motor function' without risking suffocation. A big marble has some great advantages over indoor golf balls. Unlike my sister's favourite big ball, a marble has a lot of mass in a small space. When you have one of these in your hand you really know you have something there. It is hard, heavy and cold and usually tastes of whatever it has been near recently. When they have been in my pocket they are warm. When they have been hanging in the marble bag over the radiator in my bedroom in winter, they can get quite hot. Little indoor golf balls seem to be the same whatever the weather and are slightly monotonous – but safe. They do have the fascinating property of allowing your fingers to become jammed on the holes, however, so I put up with them. I even managed to get the tip of my tongue wedged in one once, much to my sister's amusement.

For about a minute I once had a giant marble which cost a pound from an arts centre and was the densest thing I had ever felt in so small a space but it rolled away and was gathered up by whoever it belonged to. I have never worked out how to have another go with it.

I think perhaps I am unlucky to have been born in the age of plastics because most plastics, especially the kind most toys are made of, are as boring as the indoor golf ball (real golf balls are excellent). I think it must be that plastic can be made to *look* wonderful. Indeed, Trudy once told my mum that the colours on plastic toys are so bright that children find it difficult to notice other features.

See Simone Webb (1994): she points out that young children can never seem to do sequencing games with stacking cups and such, because the colours are so strident that the small differences in size are hard to notice. If a set of nesting cups were all the same colour then their relative sizes would be more easily studied.

We were playing with a set of nesting tins at the time. The smallest only held one marble. We were comparing the sizes of the tins by counting the number of marbles that fitted in them. This is one of the few times when I thought that to be blind was an advantage as I could not see the irrelevant colours.

My uncle Tim says I am lucky to be free from the seduction of advertising – so perhaps there are two advantages. He says that George Orwell says that advertising is the sound of a stick in a swill bucket. That sounds like a good sound to me but I suppose he is right in a way. Some of my classmates get quite excited when they hear their favourite advertising jingle broadcast but I suspect it is a sort of effortlessness that appeals; they don't have to do any real listening.

One of my close associates is addicted to one particular tape and can kick up such a fuss to hear it that he can avoid all the tasks he doesn't want to take part in! It's his sort of comfort blanket. Indeed, he can blanket out almost anything with his clamouring. He is particularly good at blanketing out things I am trying to attend to. So far I've only managed to bite him once but I have noticed staff are getting less vigilant recently, so I may get another chance soon.

I used to have a reputation for biting. It was one of my earliest strategies for communicating 'No thank you' or 'Go away'. I now have a more sophisticated sign which is turning my head away. People are not always good at receiving this signal; I think it depends on whether they are attending in my direction, so I now check to see if their voice or breathing is wafting towards me rather than away before doing my turning. In the days when I hadn't worked out how people could detect my movements even when they weren't close to me, I used to wait until they were very close before I showed my refusal, which is how the teeth came in. I always have them handy for special occasions when people are being especially dim.

Occasionally sighted people appear to be totally unaware of certain things. I have discovered that this has to do with transparent and opaque. They cannot see inside my body and through my clothes, for example. I have 'seen through' my grandfather's game of feeling my tummy and pretending to be able to feel what I have just eaten, though for years I assumed people would be able to see such things.

Nowadays I have four rather good statements which most people have worked out or have had explained to them. My first is a sort of humming 'myongg' which means 'Stay with me', the head turn and stopping humming mean 'Go away' or 'No more of this', and I have a rather engaging croaking cry for 'Do it again'. The croak usually startles me with its force and I go into a full body muscular spasm which in turn startles some people who are distracted and forget to find out what it is I am asking for. At this moment they see me as spastic rather than conversational.

Helen Bradley points out that children need to be able to utter four distinct statements if they are to gain some control of their lives:

stay with me	leave me alone
give me more of this activity	give me less of this activity

This appears in her *Assessing Communication Together* binder (1989) and is a useful quadrant to bear in mind when people with compound disabilities don't seem to be offering much in the way of communication at all. Staff and families can begin responding to any old movement or noise as if it were intentional communication in the hope that the penny will drop and the person can use these movements and sounds in order to communicate intentionally. Before she can do this she has to find out that someone is out there reading her signals.

In Rita Carter's *Mapping the Mind* (1998: 12) there is an account of an observation of two different brain activities which occur when a person *obeys* an instruction to move or *decides* to make the movement. In the first example, the spoken command is processed in the language area of the brain and the movement is directed from the motor area – the example is 'Raise your middle finger', but when the person is told to choose which finger to raise, a new chunk of the brain lights up to make the choice and decision to move. In the context of child development, *intending* to do something might be one definition of what play is. Co-operating, on the other hand, is passive; self-initiated play is activity and evidence of the very sense of self (see the reference to Winnicott below). In the literature on deafblind children there are many references to 'intentionality' which is an objective that teachers want their pupils to achieve: as with autistic people, they have a problem identifying other people's intentions and need to manage their own intentions alongside the conflicting intentions of their peers – no small task as every 2-year-old's tantrums will show!

Another source of information on this process might be found in the literature on Transactional Analysis, such as Ian Stewart and Vann Joines's *TA Today: A New Introduction to Transactional Analysis* (1987). In this tradition the child is seen to have to adapt to the demands of others, mainly parents, and so her urges are socialized. Children often intend to do one thing only to find they are thwarted and battles or negotiations between themselves and others ('intersubjectivity': each has to have a sense of self) ensue.

D. W. Winnicott (1990: 156) warns parents 'There will be this long tussle which you will need to survive' and for those among you who smugly think you are through that, remember you have yet to weather the 'ordinary turbulence' of adolescence (Dartington 1995: 253–61).

In a nutshell
- Stereotyped movements were perhaps once meant to communicate something and still could if only we could fathom it out; the behaviour would then change. Puzzling behaviour seems meaningless. Try interpreting it rather than setting out to eliminate it. It is probably serving a purpose.
- Playthings need to be substantial to appeal to more than just the visual sense.

Episode 10

A SENSE OF POSITION

There was one woman who worked in my school whose job I never really fathomed. She would appear in my classroom from time to time and get deeply into conversation with the teacher. I think she must have been a teacher without a class but I'm sure she wasn't the deputy or the head so I don't quite know how they wangled her post. It used to take me ages, sometimes years, to work out what everybody's role was in the school. Some I never really placed in a hierarchy and people whose place I knew would leave and be replaced without me realizing who the new person was replacing.

This teacher used to take me to another room twice each week for a couple of terms. There's another confusing thing. Rooms change their uses too and I am never consulted and am usually left to discover by accident that the speech therapist's broom cupboard is now the wheelchair store, for example.

The journey to the room was always a model of how I liked best to be moved. She studied the route carefully with me so that I knew where I was at each moment and had a good idea where I was going to end up. She had a knack of staying focused on me and always kept a hand on my shoulder but what I liked best about these journeys was the way she told me who else was around and what they were doing. It was this information that contributed to my discoveries about what sighted people can do. She could even see traffic outside but she was hopeless at telling which cars and lorries were passing. She had no problem distinguishing a bus from a lorry (I believe they look very different) but made no attempt to distinguish among lorries which I would have thought would have been easier for a sighted person than for me. She would always describe what she thought I could hear and feel but I longed to tell her about my uncle and his love of MAN diesels and Dafs.

We would come to our retreat and she worked out a way of getting me out of my chair onto the floor with me doing almost all of the work. It involved me kicking the foot rests out and then sliding down with my arms over the side panels to steady my descent. This always got me laughing and in a good mood for the real purpose of our meetings – the stories.

I forget which was the first hat I wore; it was probably the policeman's helmet (she had a real one which I hoped wasn't stolen) but gradually I had a collection of hats I was expected to choose, so that I could get my preferred story. This struck me as extraordinary. One of the reasons I had never really been keen on stories was that I had no say in what I should hear. People usually asked if I'd like one or the other but they always did the choosing in the end. They seldom offered me an object associated with the story to help me with a clue to latch onto the theme. So many of the tales were from beyond my realm of experience that I had lost interest in them by the time this teacher took me on.

I remember her getting all excited when she put the policeman's helmet on the floor to one side of me, and the milkman's peaked cap on the other side. My job was to indicate which one I preferred by making some sort of movement to the right or left. I had been hoping for the postman story as I liked the bit where he got chased by a dog. I pondered how I could ask for one that wasn't on offer whose hat was still in the box on the settee in the little bay window. I twisted my head and trunk towards the general direction where I thought they were. The teacher was disappointed that I wasn't doing my nice neat arm flap on the left or right; instead I was writhing about. Fortunately she was one of those rare birds who only asked me the kind of questions I stood some chance of answering and, what's more, she gave me time to organize my response without bombarding me with more questions that got in the way of the first question I was trying to deal with. She observed my movements, saying 'So you don't want either of those?' which I thought was pretty good. She was amazed that I had worked out that there was a collection in a box in a certain place. She went through the box and laid hat after hat before me until we settled on the posty. I was so excited I flapped everything, abandoning any left/right notion. There was no hope of my moving only one arm and the teacher realized this and pressed on with the story.

I got a special treat that day. After the session we went via the caretaker's flat and provoked the dog into barking and chasing us. It was a very small dog with a high-pitched yelp that Rosemary hated and when we got back to the classroom Rosemary was apoplectic with anguish at the noise of the irate dog. I was thrilled and resolved to provoke the dog for Rosemary as often as I could. I perfected a high-pitched squeal which always got Tufty incensed as I passed by, with the inevitable consequence that Rosemary was inconsolable. Wonderful.

This story selection routine was devised by Heather Murdoch when she taught at RNIB Rushton Hall School. She is the same person I mentioned before who went on to tutor at Birmingham University in deafblind children's education and has published books and many articles.

In a nutshell
- The journey to and from the activity is also an activity in its own right, worthy of fine attention.
- Simple routines need to be invented enabling a student with limited communication skills to make choices.
- Even people with severe and compound disabilities can make mischief.

Episode 11

A SENSE OF TEXTURE

Sometimes I have great difficulty eating and cannot enjoy what I am offered even when I like the food available. If I am not hungry, people sometimes wrongly assume that I do not like what is on offer and they pass the word around that I do not like something.

Peanut butter is my latest mistake. It has long been a favourite because it sticks to the roof of my mouth and I can enjoy it for hours after a meal. One of my teachers had an assistant who used to scrape food off the roof of my mouth and ruin this particular private pleasure. (I have since learned that food stored this way causes tooth decay but it seems a shame, especially as I am unable to grab peanut butter for myself whenever I fancy some.)

The most recent occasion was when I had had some raisins which are quite interesting to have in your mouth. I can do certain things with my tongue and teeth that enable me to get some juices going and I can even keep most of it in my mouth long enough to swallow almost all the bits. My helper at school had been giving me raisins at snack time and then tried peanut butter on toast fingers. Now my successful tongue–tooth movement for raisins doesn't work with peanut butter on toast. That requires a quite different movement. I had spluttered at the toast because I was still processing the raisins, not because I didn't like the next flavour. She never offers me peanut butter on toast any more.

This problem with textures arises almost daily when I am tackling things that come with custard; everyone seems to think that if they whack in a bit of liquid it'll help the solids down. That's not how it works for me. My way of dealing with custard is to suck and swallow but I can't do that with date sponge; it needs working on. I like to take my time with the sponge then have a slurp of the custard and so on alternately. My mum is the only one who seems to allow time for this. When she helps me eat she does it in a semi-comatose state while watching *EastEnders* so she kind of forgets to give me the next spoonful. Maybe it's just by accident that I get enough time. She does, however, alternate the solids and liquids because of something Trudy said on the subject. I think she'd been on a speech therapy course.

We had a mum helping in our class one day who prided herself on the skill with which she fed her child and had volunteered to tackle me. I'm a notoriously difficult person to support while I'm eating. She went to it with a will and filled my mouth with food, using the next spoonful to force the last one along the conveyor belt of my tongue. I'm familiar with this approach; it treats the mouth as an upward extension of the gut which acts just like that, squeezing food along. I think the mouth needs treating differently. It is the point at which pleasure in flavours and textures is experienced and there is some chance to interact with the helper and have some sort of discussion about the individual elements of a meal. Otherwise every meal might as well be brown Windsor soup.

We did that in a lesson once – combined all the foods in a plastic bag and massaged them; whatever we put in, it always turned out brown. The same thing happened with paints: as soon as many colours were stirred together we got brown – a tertiary, our art teacher told us (she meant three colours combined). Food is not paint and needs to be savoured individually. I like to have my dinner shovelled in but one thing at a time so that I can understand what I have eaten. This is a silver rather than a golden rule as I don't think cheese on toast would be much good separated into its constituent parts!

April Winstock in *The Practical Management of Eating and Drinking Difficulties in Children* (1994) writes about 'supporting people's eating' rather than feeding as her phrase is less demeaning to the person whose meal it is. Feeding is what we do to babies and animals but our job as workers with people with disabilities is to see that the person who is eating is the active one. In her workshops April has people eating raisins and custard in order to appreciate the different mouth actions needed to process the different consistencies. Have someone 'feed' you with each one and both combined and experience the sensation.

In a nutshell

- Eating is complicated. Make it simpler by offering one texture at a time. Observe the eater closely so that opportunities to communicate are not missed.
- Name the foods being experienced.
- A refusal may be for many reasons. Offer it again another day.
- Allow time for the eater to indicate when she is ready for another mouthful. Watch the whole body for an indication – she may move her foot to say 'More please'.
- Try extending favourites. If peanut butter is a popular choice then vary it with cashew nut butter and other nutty or chocolate spreads and offer the jars as smells so that the person eating at least has the opportunity for indicating preferences.

Episode 12

A SENSE OF HOLDING

Trudy and my uncle had been watching a Danish video and decided to try out some more Lilli Nielsen experiments on me. We had great fun boiling a tiny pot of sugar in the microwave, dipping a stick in it and rolling it in cornflakes.

Once it had cooled, they strapped it across the palm of my hand and left me to smell it and drool. Over the next few days I had several goes at it, wondering what I was supposed to do, when suddenly it seemed to be against my lips. During one of the half-hour sessions I had been experimenting with opening and closing my hand to find out why the stick didn't drop when I released my grip (something I found difficult as well as puzzling). I had had my mind half on something else, distracted by much toing and froing, when the gnarled but sweet substance brushed against my cheek and lip. It was delicious – not just to taste, but to contemplate that it was me, aided only by a stretchy band around my hand, that had caused this event. I invented a private stratagem that sometimes got me around the obstacle of my disobedient muscles: I used to imagine where I would like the toffee to be if it were under my control – and, lo and behold, often it would mysteriously be there at my mouth! If I strained to get it there, however, it would go every which way but in.

My uncle said he was going to find a wholefood equivalent and had me sucking celery sticks, also strapped to my palm. While this is OK, it does not quite have the cachet of cornflake toffee crunch. The carrot did not appeal to me at all. A real wood liquorice chew was better and lasted all day.

The feel of the hard things in my mouth reminded me of earlier times when my mum had given me a jelly dummy to suck. She held the ring part while I sucked on the blob part. It was so much more interesting than the pulp I was usually fed. Such a treat to have something to chew and suck without anyone worrying about whether I would choke! This had led to a succession of edible things being dangled in my Little Room, right in the middle where my mouth tended to be. I got quite a kick out of pursing my lips and manoeuvring my head until I could get a purchase on the morsel. My sister said it was like apple bobbing at Halloween – only upside down. I did get a go at that once but nearly drowned in the process. Mum devised a series of gadgets to hold foods that I might enjoy by my own efforts. The peeled banana in a string bag should have been OK but it only worked when a small piece was tied into a corner of a bag for me to get it right into my mouth. Banana sort of melts and trickles through the holes. Soggy Weetabix in a muslin bag is a waste; all you get is the milk. Still, I suppose it is a way of me getting milk when I feel like it, rather than always relying on someone else to take the time to feed it to me. All of these seemed to be good exercise for my mouth motor function and I did get quite adept at co-ordinating neck and jaw and mouth in order to get at the morsels.

Some people don't like my dribble and there is one worker at my school who keeps saying 'suck and swallow' to me (and to others) almost to the exclusion of all else. She seems very boring but I am probably being unkind; she is probably really interesting when she gets onto other topics than dribble. It doesn't normally bother me but there are occasions, especially cold, windy days, when I would like a dry chin or a sheltered one. Perhaps I'll grow a beard later in life if I can manage to stop my carers shaving me.

I can smell Anthony's wet bib a mile away when it is overdue for a change. He is being researched to see if any interventions exist to remedy his dehydration; he has to have lots of drinks to stop him drying out completely. Another youngster in my class seems to be the opposite. She breathes with a rasping sound and is always having her mouth dampened or sprayed with an indoor plant mister.

In a nutshell
- Some responses take ages and ages.
- Prompts can be a form of nagging.
- Mouth activity is learned and is to be encouraged.
- Dribbling is neither good nor bad, it is morally neutral – though inconvenient. Travel-sickness pills can dry up an overproductive mouth and saliva glands can be cauterized in extreme cases.
- Salves are manufactured to ease the dry mouths of mouth breathers who cannot immediately change their behaviour.

Episode 13

A SENSE OF SMELL

We had a swimming helper who had been retired early because of some internal health problem that didn't seem to interfere with his movements at all. So he volunteered to come to our school and help with some swimming groups. He had a pet theory that some of us recognized people by their smell and so he used to slap aftershave all over so that we would recognize him. I swear the whole pool smelled of him and that there was an extra oily skin on the surface of the pool on the days that he swam.

What he didn't seem to realize was that he already had a distinctive smell for free. He was endowed with a particular musty fragrance that no amount of Brut could mask. As he had a beard, I was never sure what the aftershave was supposed to represent. Perhaps he had been shaving hidden parts; who knows? I found it all a bit confusing; indeed, there were days when he swam with me first that I felt quite nauseous. Yet he was a lovely guy and his own smell was pleasant and easy to endure. Because people make a gentle impression on my sense of smell does not mean I cannot recognize them.

People are sometimes embarrassed at smells and don't like to admit that they exude odours. I understand there are pheromones too that we excrete to excite each other sexually but I've only heard titbits of information about these and am not a great authority on them. I do detect, though, changes in people's arousal states and the way their body odours change during the course of a day and that they vary from day to day. It is sometimes nice to be with a person long enough for their added perfumes to wear off so that I can appreciate their identifying uniqueness.

Because I have spent much of my life in a wheelchair I am often near to people at crotch level, the point at which some significant olfactory messages seem to be sent. My uncle's dog seems to prefer contact with people at crotch level. He always sits with me with his nose tucked into my crotch and cats always seem to curl up there too – though I think in a cat's case it is the warmth they enjoy; they are like little heat-seeking missiles. Years ago we had a cat who would sneak into my room and snuggle round my neck. She had to be shut out as my dad decided she would suffocate me. He didn't like the way her mouth was so close to mine that we breathed each other's exhalations. I missed her and can sometimes recall the whole savour of her presence.

The bit of smells that humans seem openly to enjoy is the hot smells that waft up from the collar. They often clutch me to their necks and treat me to a blast of their heat and scent, often liberally laced with talc and assorted cosmetics. Because we are more or less sealed into our clothing I find that the collar is the main route for the escape of heat and the accompanying rain of sloughed-off skin scale (which makes up most of household dust). It often makes me sneeze which I am grateful for as I cannot blow my nose on command. I have been practising coordinating lung and diaphragm but it seems my voice and nose blowing are doomed to inactivity. Sneezes are the thing. They really clear me out and leave me able to detect the subtlest nuance of smells.

There was a time when my nose was blocked for what seemed like months. My main method for knowing who was about was blocked off and I had forgotten about it until one spring day when some pollen got at me and I was catapulted back into the richly perfumed world that had eluded me. My classmate Rosemary was permanently bunged up and can rarely have enjoyed this dimension. But since she can see, perhaps it is not so important for her. One of our classmates was admitted with what appears to have been a lifelong blockage and I hear she had mucus glands cauterized.

It is possible to be dazzled by too pungent a smell, like the swimming pool aftershave. It lingers and interferes with the next thing to radiate a smell. Everyone and everywhere seems to have a code smell. In houses, the next thing to whatever is cooking is the smell of carpets. They seem to soak up the family smells and ooze a sort of history in scent. All the rooms at my school are distinguishable by their smell and I often chuckle to myself at the efforts people sometimes make to help me identify the rooms by little signs hanging on doorknobs which are supposed to help me recognize the function of each room. The odd thing is that these functions change term by term and the signs come and go but the smell is always there. There are days when I have a little library of smells on my hands, a record of the day's events which are expunged by the next person to wash me. I wish I had a way of retaining these without becoming filthy.

The more modern a building is, the less distinctive is the aroma. It's the same with acoustics. In a modern building the rooms all sound similar but in ancient ones which have been extended and adapted over the generations there can be different flooring, different doorways, different heights and distances and of course the characteristic accumulated smell that seeps from the materials and the people within.

When I realize that I know where I am and I know who I am with it is via a combination of sensory experiences that let me know what the general picture is. I don't think to myself 'Smells like Jim, sounds like Jim, feels like Jim'; it's more like becoming aware all at once of the Jimness of him. It helps if I can hear him clomping along the corridor whistling and rearranging the keys in his pocket, but he doesn't have to emphasize these things for me to know it is him.

Now Rosemary can see him and hear him and still she does not recognize him but I have come to believe that that is not because she doesn't have the information but that she attaches no importance to it and does not remember having seen him or heard him before. Quite what we do about that is perhaps for Rosemary to write in her account of the view from her particular window. I have a hunch that she recognizes him only when he picks her up and whirls her round but it isn't so much him she recognizes as the movement he imposes on her. It doesn't seem to include a person-to-person element at all. I wonder where she is on the autistic spectrum.

We had a researcher come to our school once to see how we responded to smells and I was involved even though I couldn't tell him what I thought I was smelling. One of the so-called scents was Dirty Laundry and there was New-mown Grass. It seemed odd to me to have bottled these essences when the things themselves were plentiful (like the flavour smoky bacon). When Steven was asked what the linen smell reminded him of he replied 'Grandpa' – which seemed to amuse everyone concerned. I have met Steven's grandpa and he actually smells OK.

> Blind children's reactions to smell was the core of Roger Hinds's MSc dissertation at Warwick. He is now Wilson-Hinds and runs Choice, Technology and Training (see Appendix). The artificial smells were concocted by Avon Cosmetics for him.

Apparently the firm that made these pongs also made industrial perfumes. The one everyone but me knows and loves is the smell of freshly baked bread in the superstores which used to upset Rosemary. They waft it to us at the entrance but the bakery section is right across the shop. You have to pass all the other things for sale, drooling on your way to get at the real thing.

Rosemary perceives movement through a range of senses as she is swung around. She can sense the changing pressure of her skin against the swinger, the liquids in her inner ear slosh around with the acceleration and centrifugal force, as do all the soft and fluid-filled parts of her body. She can feel her joints move as they dangle. The proprioceptors in each muscle tell her what state they are in as they move, her vestibular sense in her ears tells her where her head is in space, her skin registers warmth and coldness as well as texture. To find out more about how all the senses need educational attention, read Flo Longhorn's *A Sensory Curriculum for Very Special People* (1988) and get hold of her range of booklets from Catalyst Education Resources (see Appendix), or go on her inspirational courses!

In a nutshell
- Olfaction, the sense of smell, is an underestimated source of information.
- A dozen or more sensory systems operate in the skin and deeper in the body tissue.
- Any one of these may be dysfunctional or underutilized.

Episode 14

A SENSE OF SIGN

New staff at school used to study some sort of communication system. It always baffled me. It had something to do with hands and faces and seemed to be an exaggerated form of the natural gestures and expressions which sighted, able-bodied people use all the time.

I had one teacher who was convinced I was deaf and used to tap my fingers in a complex rhythm which apparently was spelling out each word on my fingers. Unfortunately my sense of touch isn't too good and that may be the reason I couldn't tell which message he was sending me by this method. Fortunately he always spoke while he was finger-spelling, so I got the message. Whether it was finger-spelling or speech, I was the receiver of people's messages but I was unable to respond in like manner. Trudy says that if it's one-way then it isn't communication at all and only my arm flapping to make choices really counts as communication.

In most classes there were sessions several times a day when conversations went on with the hand contact/mime sort of system, but usually I was given something else to do at these times as I was apparently not profiting from them. I kind of agreed at the time but nevertheless I didn't like being excluded. I usually managed to get the gist of what was going on – true, the effort wasn't always worth it as the content was often trivial, to say the least. Like the silly 'Good morning' ritual which involved sweeping an arm for the word 'everyone' which I understood anyway without sweeping my arm around.

There was one period when I was put on my platform with the box over me from which dangled the usual selection of hardware for me to clonk. I had a helper who would sit and watch and say things like 'Clever boy, you've found the soap dish', and 'Good reaching to the left'. She could keep this up for ages. There was one occasion when she nodded off after I had managed to play dead for a few minutes. I was then able to hear what the others were up to. I heard her discuss with my teacher later that I was bored with the Little Room now and perhaps she could do something else with me instead. I grabbed an assortment of dangling bits and rattled my cage with a frenzy. To my teacher's credit, she decided to let me keep using my retreat space though nobody had ever registered the fact that I wanted to be involved in their signing sessions. This communication lark is fraught.

Two books and a video by Lindy McWilliam and Mary Lee, *Movement, Gesture and Sign* (1995), are available from the RNIB or the Royal Blind School in Edinburgh. They show how blind children with huge communication barriers can be offered a structured language of sign. If you ever get a chance to go to Edinburgh, do go and see their new building at Canaan Lane, tailor-made for blind children with complex disabilities. Also from Edinburgh, the university this time, Bronwen Burford once produced a super video on non-verbal communication with very special children. There is a third Edinburgh source of wonder at Moray House where Marianna Buultjens churns out reams of relevant stuff; see her comprehensive book with Stuart Aitken (Aitken and Buultjens 1992).

In a nutshell
- Signs can be adapted so they are closer to the body and involve more touch.
- What is communicated needs to be important to the person learning the system. Start with what interests her, rather than whatever appears on page one of the instruction manual.

Episode 15

A SENSE OF HEARING

One of my teachers was a classical music buff and used to play us an amazing selection of stuff. She was obviously keen on the harpsichord and organs. I remember longing to be able to say Buxtehude. I lay in bed at night wondering about it but I had no idea how the sounds were made. I have since found out that talkers make the B sound with their lips together and the x at the back of their mouths but I can't get my tongue and jaw and lips coordinated with my breath so I have a special groan that is Buxtehude but so far I don't know anybody who recognizes it. My gran got close once. She said 'Ooh, he likes that organ music' and she bought me an awful CD of thirties dance music on a theatre organ which fortunately I only had to listen to occasionally when round at her house. Sometimes she forgot, which was a blessing.

I find it very hard to have my choice of music played anywhere and I have become an unwilling expert in whatever current fads are about because of my sister's enthusiasm for boy bands and garage music – there's no accounting for some people's taste. I've tried looking depressed and slumped in my chair but she thinks I'm relaxed and enjoying it. I look back on the year I had with the music fan and see it as a sort of golden age of sound – though even then there were some awful moments of opera which I found a bit much.

Now, live music I can stand in any form, especially if I get to meet the musicians and they let me close to their instruments. I was amazed the first time I was pressed against an electric piano and found it was all cheating: the things I could hear weren't really there at all. I began to doubt the authenticity of lots of sounds and got a new understanding about the deception of recordings. The trouble is, I am surrounded by good quality systems that can fool me easily into thinking something is near me when it isn't – just a recording. Voices are as bad. They come at me from all angles and half the time there's nobody there!

I can cope with radio OK because I can hear that it is a machine and that every station has particular hisses and hums that tell me which one I'm listening to. My uncle reckons when we go digital all that will be evened out and they'll all be like CDs, then I won't be able to tell which station we're tuned to.

I'm very keen on Radio 4. Most of what I know comes from there. I sort of get wind of things before I'm taught them at school. Dare I say that *Woman's Hour* is my favourite? I love the weekend highlights that have started but we don't always have it on. Things are looking up though. Trudy has been over with a switch system connected to a radio with an automatic tuning button and she has been showing me how to nod onto the switch to change the channel. So far all we've done is play with the switchableness of it; she wouldn't let me listen to what I'd chosen. I'm hoping she'll be back with it so I can find Radio 3 and maybe even catch some Buxtehude. How do people tell what is going to be on? I've heard a lot about the *Radio Times* but I've no idea how you get a copy or find out from it what's on. I have a hunch it's about literacy but I haven't had a chance to tackle that yet as I can't see print and my fingers can't feel Braille so I'm very reliant on hearing what's said or just hoping for pot luck.

I was at a quiz night recently where I knew all the answers to the music bit and would have won a pint of bitter if only I could have told someone the answers; not that I like bitter anyway. I was surprised how little people seemed to remember about tunes and the musicians. I think it's a problem sighted people have because they are taken in by the look of things rather than the sound and they seem to be doing other things while music is on rather than concentrating on the peculiarities of the recording. It certainly happens in shops. Most of those have awful wobbly music on tinny speakers but everyone I go shopping with seems to ignore it entirely and focus on the things that are for sale. I can go in and out of shops and not even find out what sort of place it was – though I can often tell by the smell.

Rosemary is odd about shops. She gets undressed at the front door of Marks & Spencer when the hot air blower is blasting away at the entrance. Our teacher got them to switch it off a few moments before we arrived only to find that Rosemary hates coconut matting and threw herself about in a frenzy because the floor was unsafe. Her mum won't take her shopping but our teachers are a bit more brazen in public. I suppose it's less embarrassing when the child isn't your own.

We nearly had a stand-up fight with a bloke who was tearing our teacher off a strip for not controlling Rosemary properly so that's when we started to carry those cards with our phone number on it and a brief explanation of Rosemary's problems so that we don't have to stop and explain why things fall over in shops when Rosemary is about. Actually, she has improved enormously recently.

My uncle sniggers at people who say 'actually'. Perhaps it's as well I don't speak or I'd probably fall out with him. All that time listening to Radio 4 has got me thinking in BBC English! I was glad to discover recently that my uncle's speech is a perfectly good way of communicating; it just isn't standard English. An American was telling us that standard English is just another dialect – but it has an army and a navy (meaning, it's the dominant dialect) so it's the one that gets used for writing and formal occasions, not because it's better or more correct. It's a relief to find that out. I'd come to believe that my uncle was common and therefore so was I. I prefer to think of us as variants now. Come to think of it, I suppose my disabilities are just a variation too. Mind you, it doesn't make movement any easier (or any *the* easier as my Welsh friend would say. She it was who told me that all this education didn't make you any the nicer. Sobering thought.)

In a nutshell

- Careful observation can often reveal the preferences of a person who cannot indicate them in a standard fashion.
- Expose children to a range of sound experiences in order to establish what it is they are interested in.
- Help them make choices with switches or low-tech interpersonal means – you may be their only chance.

Episode 16

A SENSE OF MOVEMENT

One of my teachers went on a course on mobility. Usually this means trotting around with a blindfold on and a white cane or a sighted guide and then eating a meal. But this course was specially for people working with children who do not walk and cannot feed themselves. My physiotherapist uses the word mobility when he's testing how far my joints will move in their sockets but this was to do with going places.

> The longer (two year, qualification) courses in mobility and orientation tend to be combined with rehabilitation and they focus on the needs of adults and elderly people needing to adjust to sight loss. Extra modules are sometimes offered on children's mobility. It is quite a different matter to consider how a child who has never seen will learn how to map her environment from considering how a newly blinded adult converts her visual map of the world to the new circumstances. Children will spontaneously invent strategies and are not normally struggling with traumas associated with loss. Guide Dogs for the Blind offer such training.

She came back all charged up with exciting things to tell me and try out. She had long known that I could hotch myself forwards in my wheelchair when I wanted to get at what was on the table and that I could kick myself away from things I did not want to use.

Her course tutor was invited to our classroom and they discussed me and my movement problems. I was fascinated. My teacher was beside herself with delight that, the day before he came, I had got hold of a table and whizzed myself towards the door. For me to be able to do this she had had to break the school rule that children in wheelchairs must always have their brakes on when stationary.

I was supposed to demonstrate what I had done but I couldn't remember how I had done it. Once I was shown the table and my hand placed on its corner, I managed to produce a similar movement with a sort of spasm that felt nevertheless as if it was really me that was in control. I swept myself backwards towards the doorway. I could then hook my hand round the edge of the door and propel myself backwards through it. My teacher turned me away from the entrance hall and I sped backwards to the head's office and got myself inside with the same motion of grabbing the door and flipping in reverse.

'What do we do about this problem?' the head and my teacher chorused. 'What problem?' asked the mobility man. He was as pleased as Jean with my self-propelled journey but not at all worried that I had only managed it backwards. They agreed that, as I wasn't using sight to decide how to steer myself, it didn't really matter at this stage which way I was facing.

I thought it would be a good way of using staff time if they were all to do a course like Jean's and adopt some of the ideas I had heard them discuss. I was delighted when the head suggested a staff development day and they made a date. I found out later that it was all to happen on a day when the children weren't in school which was a shame as I would have liked to have been there.

I had had help in getting around corners and they decided I needed something to grasp that I could swing myself around by. They thought a cupboard door handle screwed to the scuff rail would do. When my teacher's daughter came and screwed some at strategic points they couldn't get me to use them at all and ended up eventually fixing great chunks of wood at each point so that I didn't have to use grip but could get a purchase on it and sling-shot myself at great force in the direction I planned to go and into whoever was coming the other way.

As I didn't know whether I was about to collide with anyone (and there are some fairly rickety people around my school), I tended to practise this new skill when everyone else was in class.

There was some pessimistic talk of getting me assessed for an electric wheelchair as my urge to travel probably would outstrip my ability to get to the places I wanted. Not many blind children have been equipped with powered chairs, though I heard about schools and families who had bought their own at huge expense. Sometimes, our visitor told us, the money is wasted and the child cannot manage them. That must be so frustrating for all concerned.

I thought it would be good if we could go somewhere and try all the different kinds out.

When we talked to my parents about all this they were surprised. I hadn't shown any desire to move around at home. Our visitor agreed with me that homes are too small for whizzing about in and carpets make it much more difficult to get rolling.

We had a hilarious session in the school hall where my dad built a garage out of three wooden-backed crash mats, precariously balanced against the wall bars, soft sides in. My job was to steer Anthony's borrowed electric-powered wheelchair into it. By some fluke I pressed the joystick at such an angle that I shot off in a curve that brought me exactly to the entrance, into the structure and into the side wall so that the three sections collapsed on top of me (that's why I told you they were soft sides in, so you wouldn't fret).

I remember my mum saying that the PE teacher was not amused. He had been barking orders at me to turn left, press the lever, stop, and so on and was worried I might chip something. I had no idea how to respond to his directives as I hadn't then worked out where left was and which action on the joystick resulted in which changes of direction and speed. Everybody else was amused at my antics, fortunately. They gave me lots of goes but I couldn't reproduce that first heady success. The caretaker thought I would just bend things if let loose with one of those gadgets – but who was asking her, anyway? Our technology teacher said we could have tracks down the corridors for the chair to follow automatically with sensors. Sounded a bit *Tomorrow's World* to me. I reckon I could drive along corridors if they had neon lights along them. I find they are just discernible enough for me to tell where I'm headed and I could make good use of them with a bit of practice. It's annoying when strip lights are arranged in rows which don't seem to relate to the layout of the room.

What with sliding in and out of my chair to the floor and demolishing makeshift garages, I'm becoming a force to be reckoned with.

My second attempt in Anthony's borrowed chair involved bubble packing. We had yards of it all rolled up in one of the store cupboards. (Apparently the head teacher goes in there after tricky meetings and bursts bubbles therapeutically, but I'm not supposed to know that.) Rolled out on the floor it is a great incentive to run and jump, or, in my case, to flatten it with the wheels of the Merc (as Anthony's escort calls his chair).

It was a bit like fireworks night and if I could keep going in a straight line I got to burst hundreds of the bubbles with very little effort, just a forward pressure on the joystick. Our mobility visitor thought I might have trouble realizing that the one stick could be the means of reversing, rolling forward and turning either left or right, and plans were drawn up to have different switches on my tray so that I could reach to the left to turn to the left, the right to turn right and forward and back to move in those ways.

I was more interested in what I had to press to get to the car park. At that time I didn't know that to get there I had to perform a precise series of forwards, lefts and rights. But I was getting there. When the team realized that my work in the hall was centred in my mind on how to get out of it, they brought me to the doorway and I discovered that any deviation from the middle way brought me up against posts to either side. I had never encountered these before and needed time to be left to bang into them until I had registered their position and importance. I was then allowed to edge along a corridor demolishing stands of sticks and the signing-in table – which I also had never encountered before.

My trail of destruction for them was a trail of discovery for me and seemed to bear no relation to all the other times I had travelled these routes with someone else at the helm, skilfully depriving me of knowledge about door frames and furniture in the corridors.

We soon discovered that my interest in moving around and exploring the limits of my school environment transferred to my ordinary wheelchair and I was soon supplied with one with wheels that I could get my hands on and propel. Until that point, most people treated me like a marrow in a wheelbarrow, an object to be transported hither and thither. Some folk to this day behave as if speed is of the essence and they whisk me places in a trice. Usually I then have to sit around waiting. I might just as well have done it myself slowly and kept fit at the same time. It's quite calorie consuming. Long ago I didn't mind being left in limbo to wait but nowadays I expect to have something to occupy me.

The first person to tackle this waiting issue sensibly was in a class where my helper always wheeled me to a corner where there was a bead curtain and varying collections dangling. He would always plonk me within arm's reach of these so that I could create a little harmless havoc in the hiatus between events. The teacher would rotate different displays on themes the class were working on and I could have a go at clattering the bits and pieces that were soon to be discussed in the curriculum-oriented sessions. When I was offered a bowl and a spoon to stir with, I had already had bowls and spoons to bang and rattle and was at least familiar with part of the process.

My favourite wet lunchtime was when a classroom assistant tied a string around my wrist and tied that to a seaside display hanging from the ceiling in a vast net that nearly filled the classroom. I hadn't known it was there before but it seethed with activity once I yanked the string. Everyone wanted a go until Peter, who has challenging behaviour, managed to pull it hard enough to bring the whole thing crashing down. I haven't been allowed another turn as a result. I am not keen on Peter, or the people who decide that his roughness means I can't have another go.

The mobility man sparked off a few new routines in our class. He told us about a school he had just been to where lots of the kids had standing frames like me. The teacher decided her pupils were too isolated when they were clamped in them and, even with bowls let into the trays for them to dabble their hands in, they weren't able to socialize around an activity in the way other children do. Sand is OK but sand and a friend is much better and gives you somewhere to aim with the spoonfuls. Anthony and I tried out the new plan and were clamped to frames set opposite each other so that we were both over the same tray.

Sometimes we got ourselves into some odd tangles with four flailing limbs, especially in our favourite game, hockey, where we had to bash a heavy drum about the tray and hit a bell or a gong as goals. Neither of us kept a count and that way we never lost a match. The hockey element was really a cover for a wrestling bout.

Whenever the staff joined in, one of us always lost. Apparently it was essential to find out who had lost and won because then we could have a tick for doing mathematics. So that's all right then.

> Linda Bidabe found that people who seemed not to see started using their vision once they were up at the same level as other people. The Disability Partnership sell her range of MOVE Curriculum items and an instruction video (see Appendix).

On my recent voyages of discovery I have found that I have distinct preferences for who pushes my wheelchair. Those people who think of me as an object to be moved from one position to another are different from the ones who treat me as a person with perceptions; still others have a deeper respect for me as the traveller – they remember whose journey this is. My favourite is the person who sees herself or himself as my power source and takes me where I would have gone had I been independently mobile. These people come from the 'whose journey is this anyway?' category and are an occasional stroke of luck.

The approach that involves and respects me is the one that retains an interpersonal dimension. This is where the person of power speaks into my ear rather than over my head and uses my shoulders and back as a purchase for swivelling me around my corners. They even announce left and right turns, tell me when I am moving and announce when I am stopping. It is often difficult to sense such things, especially when the person is tentative and creeps around so that I cannot use my body fluids to feel the centrifugal force of a decent turn, acceleration or deceleration. When they get it right, I can perceive the course or map of my journey. The proof of this came as a moment of enlightenment when I was being negotiated upstairs in a community centre and realized I must be over the restaurant (a rather grand name for the tinpot cafe that Hector runs). I knew it wasn't the smell that told me where I was; it was definitely an intellectual reasoning of some sort that enabled me to get my bearings. Downstairs is easy as there is the ramp to the door, the crash through the swing doors onto lino, the rattle of the inspection cover, an inlaid straw mat between the garden door and the cafe, followed by the concrete bit and then carpet and stench of whatever has been keeping warm all morning for our delectation and delight at lunchtime.

The upstairs of big buildings have fewer cues than downstairs but journeys all have a specific time and speed for me to estimate distances. In this centre, the distance to and from the lift, which appears to have been installed for my individual use, takes a number of seconds which help me use this landmark to beat all landmarks.

To go back to the swing doors and crashes, my power sources also divide into two other groups: those who involve me in negotiating doors and other obstacles and those who use my chair as the tool to operate such hazards. They hook my chariot onto the door edge, give me a quick flick left or right and hurl me forward before either of us is caught on the rebound. Any premises that have been upgraded to satisfy fire-precautions neurotics have a wonderful array of spring-loaded hurdles I must overcome. They are excellent markers of my progress but can, in the wrong hands, be the points of my frequent disorientation. If I am used to propel them aside, then the left and right flicks completely foul up my mental map and I end up surprised at where I have ended up. The route is unfathomable. Maybe it's like the squash court where on my first visits I kept encountering loads of rattly doors before I realized it wasn't loads but one door reappearing.

We had a visiting Pole as a volunteer at a family holiday we all went on once and he kept taking me around a rectangular room until I got the point that it was four-sided and then he took me across the diagonal in order that I should appreciate that such spaces are not linear but three-dimensional. We played with a metal board with triangular magnets on it so that we should arrive at the geometric reality of short cuts across spaces. This worked fine for those with legs and purposeful movement but I was left with the words that I can recite to you but not the full sense of what he was driving at.

Boguslaw Marek, a professor of linguistics at the Catholic University of Lublin in Poland, markets 'hungry fingers' materials to assist blind children in forming useful concepts. See Appendix for contact address.

There is another way of surprising and confusing me, and that is to swap pushers en route without mentioning it to me. I used to work hard at keeping in mind the identity of people, even quiet people, and it was easy to spring sudden switches on me and cheat me into believing that people just magically appear and disappear.

In a nutshell
- When a wheelchair user is transported she is passive. When she is propelling herself she is active. The active state implies learning and knowing and is educational. Passivity is the curse of special education.

Episode 17

A SENSE OF FAR AWAY

My dad used to take me to the airport near us to get me ready for a package holiday we were embarking on. He thought I would need acclimatizing to all the new sounds and sensations of foreign travel. After a couple of trips there, we got invited to go into an aeroplane that was waiting for a delayed crew and I even got to the flight deck and had earphones on my head connected to air traffic control! A steward gave me the smallest can of cola I'd ever held but when I drank it, it had just the same effect as a big one and made swallowing rather hazardous.

I had a taste of the international scene before I ever got abroad on holiday. We had two visitors from South Africa in our classroom, one who talked non-stop and one who, like me, never spoke at all. The quiet one was a little girl who sat by me and rolled on top of me, laughing and dribbling and prodding me with stumps instead of hands and banging me with the crash helmet she wore on her head. She was trying out my Little Room and resonance platform at the same time as I was trying to do some serious playwork in it. Something about it tickled her sense of humour and interested the talker. The talker treated me as if I understood every word she said, which I did almost, and I learned how the child had been burned (I knew what that was) in a shanty town fire (I didn't know what that was). She had had her eyelids, nose, lips and fingers burnt off (each of which I kind of understood but found hard to make sense of). I know my teacher understood because she now has a Children of Fire tin in our kitchen corner which staff put money in if ever they burn anything or themselves (they haven't managed to burn any of us yet – that should raise a tidy sum if they do!).

When Libby Purvis spoke to them on *Midweek* on Radio 4, our class all listened. I thought it was interesting how one of the other guests was wary of Dorah at first but discovered that he could relate to her as just a little girl who liked to wrestle with friendly people.

Children of Fire International supports Dorah Mokoena and other burn victims identified by Bronwen Jones as needing plastic surgery or other help. She also organizes fire prevention work in squatter camps, literacy support and school, and other campaigning around burned children's issues in southern Africa. See Appendix for details.

In a nutshell
- People blind from birth are referred to as congenitally blind; those blinded later in life, adventitiously blind. The implications for each are different.

Adventitiously blinded people may have visual memory, though Professor John Hull who wrote *Touching the Rock* and went blind in his teens tells how his portrait gallery of people's faces is fading; though he can picture the frames he can no longer see the faces in them. A friend once told me that her only visual memory is of a dish of raw liver her mother brought out of the pantry shortly before she lost her sight at age 7.

There is a day centre in Belgium where some of the users were born deafblind, some were born blind and went deaf later, some were born deaf and went blind later, some lost sight and hearing later in life. They all have distinct needs and communication systems yet are brought together as if all deafblind people are alike. When McInnes and Treffry wrote their Canadian text *Deaf-blind Infants and Children* (1982), they observed that the only thing they have in common is their uniqueness!

Episode 18

A SENSE OF MORTALITY

Am I fortunate in having parents who are not interested in shielding me from the harsher aspects of reality? Take death, for instance. When my sister's guinea pig died I was taken out to the cage and was given the dead body to hold. I had never been keen on furry creatures though it was always my job to hold Filbert on my lap while my sister shovelled out malodorous substance 17 (in my classification). I was never quite sure where Filbert with his fuzzy outline began or ended.

When I feel my own head I reckon I begin at the scalp and that the hair is a sort of encumbrance beyond my outer limit. With guinea pigs and most other similar animals, it is harder to get to the scalp; the fur is integral but somehow is not a clear boundary between air and the thing itself. Fur toys are also indistinct in this way. I prefer to have nothing to do with them. My grandmother did not appreciate this.

Whenever we stayed there she produced an enormous Uncle Bulgaria. I think she had been the eleventh person to win it in a raffle but the first not to give it to another raffle for recycling. One of its previous owners was a smoker, another used lavender; there were the traces of many past residences deep in the fur. It got stuck with me or I got stuck with it. I quite liked the face, glasses and waistcoat but couldn't get on with the rest of the body. I had to sleep with him nevertheless. In one way it was useful because when I woke up and couldn't remember where I was, there was Uncle Bulgaria tucked in beside me and I knew straight away I was at Grandma's.

The feeling of such a toy and a dead guinea pig are uncannily alike but there is something hard about the dead thing, and heavy. Toys are almost never heavy enough to be convincing.

When Grandma died I was allowed to touch her too just to make sure I had got the idea that I was never going to hear her again or eat her food. Everything in the room and house that day smelt strange.

She had been a great bedtime singer. I have a tape of her songs which my mum can't bear to listen to but my uncle puts on for me. He has rigged up a pressure switch so that I can switch it on and off by rocking my head to the right. If I hear Mum coming, I switch it off and on again when she goes so I can remember privately the bedtimes with my lovely grandma and the not so lovely Uncle Bulgaria.

I inherited Uncle Bulgaria. I think he is on a high shelf by my wardrobe – there is a dead spot there with no echoes. If ever he is put into bed with me I have now acquired the knack of elbowing him out, otherwise I might wake up and think I've gone back to Grandma's.

One of the other deaths I've been involved in was a terrapin in our classroom. This was my first introduction to decay. Another malodour for my collection. We gave it a decent burial, suitably sombre – except for Anthony who kept giggling. I think it had probably passed on to wherever terrapins pass on to on the previous Friday. By the time we got to school the next Monday he was well past his sell-by date, as one of our classroom support workers irreverently put it.

Now terrapins are easier to master. They begin and end nice and crisply and waggle their legs slowly enough not to make me jump. I do squirm a bit, but not as much as when I was given a South American millipede that crawled across my arm. The irreverent class-room assistant did more than squirm on that occasion; she had to be helped from the room feeling all peculiar.

My favourite animal is a certain cow, not cows in general. We only met once but I shall always remember her and her rumblings. The class were visiting one of those farm parks and I was not well after the journey and not in the mood for miles of cage fronts and assorted malodours.

My teacher could tell that I was not going to enjoy the zoo trip so she took me onto a field and slid me out of my chair where she leant me against the flank of a seated cow which was chewing the cud. Have you ever heard ruminants bring up their food and give it another chew? I can see why thoughtful people are said to ruminate while they ponder things quietly and 'chew them over'.

Emily and I sat together for the whole of the visit. Her flank was vast. I suppose that is the only bit of her that I really know – though I know the words for all the other bits. Her ribs were as long as me and the leather of her skin was pungent and hot – as was her breath when she turned her head to see who was propped up against her. She put up with me for nearly an hour and I had the best farm visit I've ever had. Although she was one of the smelliest creatures I have ever experienced, I do not store the memory of her smells among the malodours: it is filed under 'E for Emily' and cross-referenced to 'cow' among the good smells or scents.

The living thing, unpackaged, rewards close inspection. My uncle won't shop in superstores on principle. He prefers to take me to the market in all weathers where I can experience each group of commodities distinctly and preferably unwrapped so that I can enjoy the variety too.

Market stall holders are always good for a gossip. Somehow Sainsbury's fruit section pales in comparison. I'm usually involved in the choosing, weighing and pouring into bags and baskets. I nearly always get samples before deciding, especially with grapes. The ones that drop off the bunch seem to provide a regular free snack for me and my uncle. He gets the job of nibbling and spitting out the skins for me.

But I was talking about death. A girl died in my classroom once and we had a memorial service. I remember the minister beginning by saying we had all met to worship Christ, and my uncle – why is it always him? – whispered in my ear that he hadn't, he'd just come to help me give Jenny a good send off so we had a really good sing.

The writer A.S. Byatt (2001) has written an eloquent essay entitled 'How we lost our sense of smell', on how our homes are saturated with smells of pine woods and forest glades in the attempt to smother the real smells of human habitation. It was first published in *Sightlines* an anthology collected by Melvyn Bragg and P.D. James for an RNIB Talking Books Appeal, published by Vintage.

In a nutshell
- Some experiences are only related in words; the event itself is kept beyond the reach of a blind child. It is worth finding a tactile back-up for the ideas being talked about.
- Some touch experiences are unsatisfactory or even unpleasant even though the materials look good.
- Conversely, some touch experiences are good and helpful even when the materials look or are thought to be unpleasant.

- First-hand knowledge is the kind most worth having.
- Packaging is a barrier to understanding to a person with impaired vision.
- It is not often useful to shield children from harsh realities.
- Smells are an imprecise source of information and have recently become misleading because of the artificial smells industry.

Episode 19

A SENSE OF SEEING

There has been a recent development in the way I get to know about what is happening out there in the world. It began in a cafe where my uncle had decided to experiment with a new feeding technique. My sister had already settled at a different table because of her embarrassment at having been seen with him ignoring the age limit sign again in the ballpool. She was glad to be away from us when he went to get a fruit juice carton with one of those bendy little straws. He had had the idea when my aunt squirted pineapple juice over herself accidentally, by holding the box too tightly. Apparently the juice had come out of the straw like a water pistol and drenched her neck and collar – much to my sister's amusement.

The big moment came as he approached me around the table. I flinched as he came across a sunlit window. I know now, after hearing Trudy and my mum discussing it, that this meant my uncle was silhouetted against the big bright window and was casting a shadow on my face. He noticed my sudden reflex movement and went back a step, moved across again and saw me react to the difference between the sunlight and the dark of his shadow. He gave a triumphant whoop, pranced about waving my drink and had me opening my mouth as he brought it near. It wasn't until I decided to ignore him that he remembered I was supposed to be getting a drink and the little fountain of juice worked quite well – though my collar and neck got just as wet as they usually do at drink times. Now my aunt knows how it feels.

Trudy and my mum have been working on the implications of my uncle's discovery (though I think of it more as *my* discovery) and we have changed the way we sit at conversation times. Now Mum sits so that she is dazzled either by sunlight or by a desk lamp spotlighting her and I am supposed to be able to see her face. While I am not altogether convinced that this really works, it is true that I have got an improved sort of sense that she is there and I reached towards where I thought her mouth probably was and found my fingers between her teeth. I am pretty good at knowing where things are by other clues too, but this was definitely to do with the level of lighting, not the smell or warmth of her breath, or the sound of her voice. I knew her mouth was mobile and needed to reach to confirm what I had already come to know.

Daniel Stern describes this as a 'higher way of knowing' that is independent of which particular sense organ you use. In his book *The Interpersonal World of the Infant: A View from Psychoanalysis and Developmental Psychology* (1985) he stresses the special importance of looking at faces and seeing mouths while hearing speech. More readable versions of this heavyweight tome are his *Diary of a Baby* (1990) and *The First Relationship* (2002). *Diary of a Baby* is so good that a string quartet has been composed in honour of it!

More recently, Gopnik, Meltzoff and Kuhl have produced the miraculous *How Babies Think* (1999) (called *The Scientist in the Crib* in the USA).

Gordon Dutton (Dutton *et al.* 1996) has written and spoken about visual agnosias and cortical visual impairment in such a way as to explain how some children who appear to be very visually impaired can nevertheless respond to some visual stimuli. This can be a response that hardly seems visual at all since it passes from the eye direct to the motor cortex, bypassing the visual cortex entirely.

Now that Trudy and my mum have got their teeth into this new issue, all sorts of spin-offs are arriving. Not least, my bedroom has been redecorated in honour of this new realization that maybe I may be seeing things after all. The wall opposite my window is now a violent violet hue and the one around the window is dung brown (though that's not quite how Dad described it when he got the job of painting it on). Another wall is green and the one with the door in it is a dusky sort of yellow but the door frame is magenta and the actual door is white with a hint of apple (so I am told). It all sounds rather like one of those interior design programmes on television, but I must confess there are times when, as a result of these contrasting colours, I can deconfuse myself by thinking about the walls and realizing which way round I am facing.

I have been given an additional aid to orientation by having a neon strip light along the violet wall. The trouble is, it hums and I am never quite sure whether I can see it or just hear its starter motor ticking over. Trudy told my dad to get it fixed so that it was silent in operation but I am not sure this is within his capabilities. Mum complains that it's already crooked so what hope is there of it being silent?

Trudy wants to control all the variables so that she and my mum can do proper detective work and definitely prove that what I am doing really can be described as seeing. I am a past master at making people think I can see when in fact I am responding to sounds bouncing off things much like a bat does with its echo-location.

Trudy discovered me doing this once when she was moving me in my wheelchair and crept slowly towards a doorway. I leaned forwards to knock on it like I usually do but stopped before I did it because I realized the door was open and couldn't be knocked on. She got my mum to play with doors for a while to demonstrate that I could tell whether it was open or closed because of sounds bouncing off the closed door but different sounds drifting through from the space beyond the door if it was open. She also found out that I can accidentally bang my head on a half-open door because I cannot pick up an echo from the edge of the door. Her discovery meant a painful experience for me.

A blind chap who works with Trudy told her that his forehead is covered in ancient scars for this very reason. He makes a joke about it contributing to his baldness but I am not sure whether this is funny or not. There doesn't seem much joy associated with hurting your head, but people always seem to laugh about such things – banana skin humour I believe it is called. People make jokes about all the bumps and crashes I have in my wheelchair. They ought to try a few rides up and down kerbs and see if they still laugh. My aunt and I used to go wheelchair country dancing but she injured her knee just before I became seasick from the whirling about, so I am spared that now. I don't wish her ill but a bit of me hopes her knee won't get better.

That was another time when I wondered where I got my sense of moving from. Was it the dance hall lights or was it the liquids in my body cavity and head slurping around ? A bit of each probably.

When I went to London University's Visual Development Unit and met Janette Atkinson and her battery of tests, I believe one of her team tested my sight by threatening to slap me in the face. Her hand was on the other side of a piece of glass so that I would not blink at the rush of air, only at the sight of the rapidly approaching hand. I didn't flinch because I couldn't see it.

Any GP can refer a child to the Visual Development Unit for assessment without charge. See Appendix for address.

One of the oddest things about that visit is that I came away with a prescription for glasses even though I almost convinced them that I could not see. They found that I was very long sighted in one eye and short sighted in the other and they told Trudy and my mum (this was in the days when my mum needed her by her side at things like that) that if my brain ever did start responding to visual stimuli, I had better have a good image on my retina to start with. I don't wear glasses all the time but whenever the main point of an activity is visual, someone usually remembers to put them on, just in case. One visual experience I had there was from a camera flash; this always reaches the visual parts that other lights fail to reach. My dad rigged up some disco lights to a voice-activated switch after that visit and I can make the lights flash by screaming into the mike. It took me ages to work this out as the lights flashed at my sister's voice too and I didn't manage to separate her and my screams in order to cotton on to quite who was causing what. This is the trouble with our light room at school. I'm hardly ever in there on my own and so don't understand how most of the switches work and what their connection is to the gadgets and gizmos.

In a nutshell
- When a person with complicated sensory needs shows a response to external events, fathom out which of the senses is enabling that response; don't jump to the conclusion that it is visual.
- Total blindness is rare; people may be registered as blind yet have some vision available.
- Educationally blind usually means that the reading of print is especially problematic.
- Blindness may be a feature of the eye itself or of the way the brain functions; the visual cortex may be damaged or other structures affected by strokes, tumours or other damage. About 60 per cent of the brain is involved in various aspects of vision.
- It takes a whole battery of tests to find out about the neurology of visual impairment. The high street optician will not have the means to examine how sight works beyond the retina and into the brain.

Episode 20

A SENSE OF LOCATION

I've had some very odd outings with my uncle. By now this won't surprise you. He decided I had never been on a bus and we bought two tickets for one of those around town jaunts where you can get on and off as many times as you like. We got off at every stop and found a landmark of some kind. He decided that I would come to know the first place by the warmth and smell of the kebab takeaway shop. The owners were very polite and tolerant as we didn't buy anything; we just stood there while a few people were served and then it was time to catch the next bus.

The second stop was near a railway bridge that went over the road. We went under it and listened to the changes in sound as lorries and buses, cars and pedestrians went under it. My first experience of being under a train was shattering in a nice sort of way. It shattered my expectations and preconceptions of what it would be like. The earth moved, my head moved in sympathetic vibration. We listened for diesels and electric engines and also heard engineers working up there. It seemed to involve a lot of swearing.

There was one place we got off at where there was a park and, after a short walk and a lakeside stint, I realized it was familiar to me from car journeys – it was my park, mine and my ducks. It had taken a while for me to make the connection. I know the route in the car from the sequence of turns and stops and slopes and things but I had not appreciated that there are alternative ways of approaching it. In later weeks I discovered that the railway arch was one I had driven under many times without knowing what the sensation had been. I'd known it as a dry patch on a wet journey and a place of strange sensations in my ears – but not sound.

The kebab shop was also en route to other places I knew but was an unreliable landmark from the car as it didn't always permeate the boundary of the car and the shop wasn't always cooking and open. I have always lost track quickly of things that don't signal consistently to me of their existence. I like my brother's computer because it hums gently to me in a way that announces its presence but doesn't drown out the sound of other things and people.

The main point of my town tour bus journey was a free lunchtime concert in a vast church which I had not been to before. Typically for my uncle, we stayed on afterwards and I got to twang the strings and strike a note or two from the keyboard. It reminded me of my music therapist who used to lie me on her frightfully grand piano and improvise melodies to fit my movements when I was little. Sometimes I would lie with my feet to the low notes and my head to the high; sometimes I would lie with high notes to my left and low to my right. It made a difference to her playing. She used to entertain herself with puns about movements being both a section of music and my muscle activity. She would say things like 'This movement is entitled "Wiggly fingers of the left hand"' and create a sound to match my actions. She said I was a great conductor. She put me on the actual strings once which was spooky. It was more satisfying than the times I had spent improvising my own melodies with a Soundbeam; the results were less melodic than the improvisations of a musician.

I found out at the concert that harpsichord strings were plucked rather than hammered and the low notes had long strings, the high notes had short ones. This was quite an 'Aha!' moment and made the whole bizarre day significant in my science education which I am sure was not my teacher–uncle's intention.

I find this often to be the case; I find out things in teacherish sessions that are not the teachers' objectives. For instance, I like to find out who drinks black coffee at morning break and who smokes (that's easy) and can emerge from a lesson having sniffed out all sorts of personal data but not remember what the lesson was meant to be about.

International volunteers are my favourite group of teacher ancillaries. They always smell exotic, especially on the days when they cook their national foods in our classroom. Best of all are the sounds they make. Lots of them just chatter away to me in their native tongues. I love it when they do that. I think I know 'Ready, steady, up' in about six languages. 'Oop-la' seems to crop up in several.

In a nutshell
- Journeys can appear linear and are often free of landmarks and therefore uninteresting.
- We grow out of the need to touch everything we see but this need never fade for people who do not use sight.

Episode 21

A SENSE OF BODY

I remember with affection those visitors who used to leave my mum in a very relaxed state. We always knew how long they were staying and they always left as soon as their time was up. My mum said she knew where she was with them and some didn't even need a cup of tea. My mum once worked out how much my visitors cost her in cups of tea; she didn't bother subtracting the value of cups they gave her on our visits to them as the amount would have been laughably small.

It took a while to decide who were the people worth seeing and who weren't. The ones who left Mum in a relaxed state had seen children like me before and had lots of useful suggestions to make. One of the ones my mum weaned herself off used to say that my mum was the only real expert and she had to decide for herself what was best for me. My mum mumbled that she wished *she* got her wages for doing nothing and knowing nothing.

We used to borrow stuff from Trudy. She brought that huge wooden platform round, the one my sister painted the most amazing colours. I used to lie on it and bang my head so that everything on the board bounced. My dad sandpapered the corners to stop me getting splinters when Trudy suggested I have bare feet while playing on it. I could make things bounce by banging my feet too which Trudy said was better than banging my head. I'm not sure she was right. There's something special about head banging. On the platform, heels are as good as heads but off it, my skull provides tremendous enjoyment and I can make sounds zoom around by swinging my head vigorously from side to side. The swish of my hair (nearly all gone from the back of my head) is one of the tunes I can always play even when I have nothing at hand to play with. When I feel weightless and placeless, a few waggles and bangs of my head and I know I'm there. If I doze off and can't work out where I am for a bit, a few rubs of the back of my head and I can tell what I'm lying or sitting on.

> The Resonansplatform pioneered by Dr Lilli Nielsen is about a metre square, made of thin marine plywood on a one-inch rail around the edge so that it is springy in the middle like a drum skin. It is comfortable for helpers to sit on, too, while engaging with the child who is exploring materials.

Trudy said I should have loads of different surfaces to experiment with. Bubble packing started off as the worst. The sheet I had at school got Rachel in a fit of giggles and a long roll of it was the thing that got Anthony crawling. All it did for me was to get me rolling and protesting but my teacher was thrilled that I'd got myself off it and promptly pulled me back on it to make me roll off it again! Education comes in some strange guises – though I suppose that was physiotherapy, come to think of it, and I didn't know it would one day come into its own on that electric wheelchair day.

Now there's a strange profession. Physios are a breed apart, and they're so tough! Mark used to tell me 'This is probably going to hurt but I'm going to do it anyway' and proceed to find out how far my joints would bend. I used to let him hurt me and then shout at the point where I couldn't bend any further. He told me that I had a choice of stretching my tendons this way or going into hospital to have the tight ones slashed and stretched in plaster. He lied. I didn't have the choice; it was him and my mum. But I was glad to go along with his method. He had wonderful arms and hands and he gave me the most exhilarating piggyback rides. He said it was more fun than sitting astride a great pommel to stretch my hip tendons and prevent scissoring. He and I won the jousting on sports day in the days when 'King Arthur' had some political significance for coal miners and Mark had his face blacked for the occasion. His prize was a can of Tetley's which he shared with me afterwards when no one was looking.

I think my sister would have liked Mark. She used to slip me all sorts of taboo foods and drink. She only choked me twice. The first was crunchy peanut butter. She decided I should try it but I couldn't shift it from my throat. She explained to my dad that she thought I was probably bored with all that yoghurt and wallpaper paste stuff. My mum taught her how to get smooth peanut butter onto my tongue so that it would gradually melt and slide down easily when I was ready. The second time was Rice Krispies. They eventually became a favourite after she had been shown how to let them soak up the milk for a bit.

It made a change from the interminable Weetabix. My aunt said I would change into a Weetabix. If it weren't for the fact that it set like cement in my wheelchair I think it would get my mum's vote as the greatest foodstuff invented. She says it should come on prescription for people like me.

Mark the physio is a fitness fanatic. Trouble is, it's my fitness he's fanatical about. He even expects me to go through his routines on holidays and weekends. Everybody else gets a break, but not me. Trudy says he's as bad as Doman and Delacato (Glen Doman and Carl Delacato (1989), controversially, recommended brain stimulation and 'cross patterning' for brain injured children. See Appendix, Institute for the Achievement of Human Potential). Thank goodness my mum didn't get into that! Sidney, in my class, gets up at five to do his Human Potential stuff and as a result is asleep half the day at school. He's also been to Budapest for his spasticity and our teacher has some of the Hungarian furniture for us to grapple with. I must say the slats are easy to keep a grip on. Trudy says it's just a coincidence and the doctor who invented conductive education could only get slatted furniture in Hungary after the war as there wasn't enough timber to make the proper stuff. She says muscle memory will tide me over the odd day's missed exercises and that it should be fun for me rather than a chore. Trudy says I reach up to hit things swinging in space around me and they make a great clanging when I do whereas poor old Sidney 'rea-ches-up-in-to-the-air' for no apparent reason (except that the programme says he must, at what speed and how often).

Conductive education is a highly structured series of exercises and routines aimed at getting children with cerebral palsy to use words to attach to movements to help them master muscle flexions they are normally unaware of. Dr Peto in Budapest had remarkable successes and his approach has a worldwide reputation, with institutions in England now offering full-time education. 'Schools for parents' form a part of the regime as home exercises are an essential part of most programmes. Oakleigh School in Barnet, the Hornsey Centre and Rutland House in Nottingham are some of the experienced centres who have pioneered extending the method to apply to children who have cerebral palsy among a host of other difficulties. The Eden Foundation in Malta sets a standard under Jackie Rizzo whom many would do well to follow.

In a nutshell
- Home visitors should not be the only ones who know how long the visit is going to last.
- 'Uncooperative parents' may not deserve their reputation.
- Intensive therapeutic approaches sometimes characterize particular institutions.

A SENSE OF AGEING

My mum and dad have been taking me to see places for grown-up disabled people to live when they are old enough to leave home. I've even been to stay in a Vision Homes Association set-up in Ludlow to see how I like it and Martin Thomas has been to my house. He had met me before when I was little and seemed pleased to see me, though I can't say I remember him very clearly – there was something about the smell of his roll-ups that triggered some sort of memories and I think he may be the same chap who played Irish jigs on his guitar, but I'm not sure. Perhaps if I do move in, he will play it again and I'll know then.

What my mum likes about VHA is that it was formed by parents whose children were all visually impaired and were going to need care all their lives and that all the staff know about my very low vision and how to organize continuing education and leisure activities that will suit me. It's not like respite care where everybody else enjoys visual things – TV, shows, cinema – it's specially geared up for the likes of me and my unusual tastes.

For the address of VHA see Appendix.

My mum and dad are thinking of moving when Dad retires so they can be nearer me but, as long as they can drive, I don't really mind how near or far they are as I can only be in touch when they visit anyway. I don't find telephone contact very satisfactory even though Mum has calls well organized when I am away. She prepares a list of things to tell me and then has a brief word with whoever I'm staying with – uncle, carer or Trudy – and hangs up. Dad hates talking to me on the phone, he gets upset and then I get upset because he's upset and we get nowhere fast.

If I don't go to Ludlow I hope I get a place somewhere fairly busy and in easy reach of shops and a pub. I'm not too keen on out-of-the-way places. I like the background sounds of towns at night, the sound of milk floats before dawn and the scheduled trains and church clocks that tell you what time it is when you are awake. I like the nuclear waste train that trundles past at 2:32 every morning. I must be one of the few people who think it is a good thing. I know my uncle doesn't approve. Where would I be without him? Where would Mum and I be without Trudy? We are scaffolded by these people and stand strong within their hold. It is a gentle grasp but a steady one and I like to hold them in mind sometimes when my mind is drifting. They are an anchor too and give me the feeling that I belong, maybe not to their full culture but in a way that says my kind of living has worth and dignity. Certainly up to now it feels to me as though my life is one worth living and it will be good to live with a new set of scaffolders where people will appreciate my need to spend a little time while shopping near a till that rattles and bleeps, or in a launderette of good vibrations and scented steam – even on days when I haven't any clothes that need a wash. They may even continue my ritual of the visit to the Edinburgh Tattoo – though I think that may still be up to my uncle to organize. He hates it but loves the way I love it. Lots to look forward to.

In a nutshell
- Visually impaired people in care may get no pleasure from run-of-the-mill leisure pursuits but may develop an absorbing fascination for matters in which sighted people show little interest.
- Moving away after school is not always an option but should be explored and the pros and cons carefully weighed.

APPENDIX

Catalyst Education Resources
1A Potters Cross
Wootton
Bedfordshire
MK43 9JG

Tel/fax: 0845 127 5281
email: cerltd@attglobal.net (website help)
or: FloCatalyst@aol.com (general information)

Children of Fire International
Rebecca Wright
Secretary
Children of Fire International
Eversley Cottages
47 Houselands Road
Tonbridge
Kent
TN9 1JJ

Bronwen Jones
Children of Fire International
PO Box 1048
Auckland Park 2006
Republic of South Africa

email: firechildren@icon.co.za

Choice, Technology and Training
Roger Wilson-Hinds
7 The Rookery
Orton Wiston
Peterborough
PE2 6YT

Tel: 01733 234441
Fax: 01733 370391
email: choice.tech@btinternet.com

The Disability Partnership
Wooden Spoon House
5 Dugard Way
London
SE11 4TH

Tel: 020 7414 1494

Eden Foundation
Bulebel, Zejtun
ZTN 08
Malta

email: info@edenfoundation.com

Rainbow Centre (children)
Tel: (356) 677319/895612
Fax: (356) 691447/8

Ability Centre (adults)
Tel: (356) 673706/7
Fax: (356) 665260

Institute for the Achievement of Human Potential
8801 Stenton Avenue
Wyndmoor
PA 19038
USA

MOVE Curriculum
Linda Bidabe
Rifton
Robertsbridge
East Sussex
TN32 5DR

National Institute of Conductive education
Cannon Hill House
Russell Road
Birmingham
B13 8RD

Tel: 0121 449 1569
Fax: 0121 449 1611
email: foundation@conductive-education.org.uk

RNIB (Royal National Institute for the Blind)
PO Box 173
Peterborough
PE2 6WS

Customer Services as for **Eden Foundation** on p. 93
Tel: 0845 702 3153
Fax: 01733 37 15 55

Helpline
Tel: 0845 766 9999 (local call rates for UK callers)
Fax: 020 7388 2034
email: CServices@rnib.org.uk
(Textphone users dial 18 001
before the numbers above)

Royal Blind School
Canaan Lane
Edinburgh
EH16 5NA

Tel: 0131 667 1100
Fax: 0131 662 9700
email: office@royalblindschool.org.uk

Scope (formerly the Spastics Society)
PO Box 833
Milton Keynes
MK12 5NY

Cerebral Palsy Helpline as for **Eden Foundation** on p. 93
Tel: 0808 800 3333
9 am–9 pm weekdays
2 pm–6 pm weekends
email: cphelpline@scope.org.uk

Sense (for people with deafblindness and associated disabilities)
11–13 Clifton Terrace
Finsbury Park
London
N4 3SR

Tel: 020 7272 7774
Fax: 020 7272 6012
email: enquiries@sense.org.uk
Text: 020 7272 9648

Techno-Vision Services Ltd.
76 Bunting Road Industrial Estate
Northampton
NN2 6EE

Tel: 01604 792 777
Fax: 01604 792 726
email: info@techno-vision.co.uk

Vision Homes Association
Quadrant West
210–222 Hagley Road West
Oldbury
West Midlands
B68 0NP

Tel: 0121 434 4644

Visual Development Unit, London University
26 Bedford Way
London
WC1E 6BT

Main unit:
Visual Development Unit
Department of Psychology
University College London
Gower Street
London
WC1E 6BT

Tel: 020 7679 7574
Fax: 020 7679 7576
email: vdu@psychol.ucl.ac.uk

REFERENCES

Adams, D. and Lloyd, J. (1983) *The Meaning of Liff*. London: Pan Books, Faber and Faber.

Aitken, S. and Buultjens, M. (1992) *Vision for Doing: Assessing Functional Vision of Learners Who Are Multiply Disabled*. Edinburgh: Moray House Publications.

Alvarez, A. (1992) *Live Company: Psychotherapy with Autistic, Borderline and Deprived Children*. London: Routledge.

Berne, E. ([1964] 1968) *Games People Play*. Harmondsworth: Penguin.

Berne, E. (1973) *What Do You Say After You Say Hello?* New York: Grove Press.

Biederman, G.B., Davey, V.A., Ryder, C. and Franchi, A.S. (1994) The negative effects of positive reinforcement in teaching children with developmental delay, *Exceptional Children*, 60: 458–65.

Bowlby, J. (1951) *Maternal Care and Mental Health*. Geneva: WHO.

Bowlby, J. (1979) *The Making and Breaking of Affectional Bonds*. London: Tavistock.

Bowlby, J. (1988) *A Secure Base: Clinical Applications of Attachment Theory*. London: Routledge.

Bradley, H. (1989) *Assessing Communication Together* (loose-leaf binder). London: MHNA.

Byatt, A.S. (2001) How we lost our sense of smell, in M. Bragg and P.D. James (eds) *Sightlines*. London: Vintage.

Carey, P. (1994) *The Unusual Life of Tristan Smith*. London: Faber and Faber.

Carter, R. (1998) *Mapping the Mind*. London: Phoenix.

Coupe-O'Kane, J. and Goldbart, J. (1998) *Communication Before Speech*, 2nd edn. London: Fulton.

Dartington, A. (1995) Very brief psychodynamic counselling with young people, in J. Maitland, *Brief Counselling with Young People*. London: Routledge.

Doman, G. and Delacato, C. (2002) *Teach Your Baby to Read*. Wyndmoor, PA: Institute for the Achievement of Human Potential.

Dutton, G., Ballantyne, J., Boyd, G. *et al.* (1996) Cortical visual dysfunction in children: a clinical study, *Eye*, 10: 302–9.

Estevis, A.H. and Koenig, A.J. (1994) A cognitive approach to reducing body rocking, *Re:view*, 26: 119–25.

Field, T. (2001) *Touch*. London: MIT Press.

Foss, Brian M. (1961) *Determinants of Infant Behaviour*, vol. 4. London: Methuen.

Gopnik, A., Meltzoff, A.N. and Kuhl, P.K. (1999) *How Babies Think* (published in the USA as *The Scientist in the Crib*). London: Weidenfeld and Nicolson.

Harlow, H.F. and Harlow, M.K. (1962) Social deprivation in monkeys, *Scientific American*, 207: 136–46.

Hobson, R.P. (1993) *Autism and the Development of Mind*. Hove: Laurence Erlbaum Associates.

Hull, J.M. (1992) *Touching the Rock: An Experience of Blindness*. New York: Vintage.

Liedloff, J. (1975) *The Continuum Concept*. Harmondsworth: Penguin.

Longhorn, F. (1988) *A Sensory Curriculum for Very Special People*. London: Souvenir Press.

McHugh, E. and Pyfer, J. (1999) The development of rocking among children who are blind, *Journal of Visual Impairment and Blindness*, February: 82–95.

McInnes, J.M. and Treffry, J.A. (1982) *Deaf-blind Infants and Children*. Toronto: Oxford University Press.

McWilliam, L. and Lee, M. (1995) *Movement, Gesture and Sign* (booklets and video, recently rewritten as *Learning from the Child*). Edinburgh: Royal Blind School.

Murdoch, H. (2002) Repetitive behaviours in children with sensory impairments and multiple disabilities: deafblind review, *Sense*, vol. 30.

Nielsen, L. (1988) *Spatial Relations in Congenitally Blind Infants*. Kalundborg, DK: Refsnaesskolen (available from RNIB).

Nielsen, L. (1990) *Are You Blind?* Copenhagen: SIKON (available from RNIB).

Nielsen, L. (1992) *Space and Self*. Copenhagen: SIKON (available from RNIB).

Nielsen, L. (1997) *Functional and Instruction Scheme: The Visually*

Impaired Child's Early Abilities, Behaviour, Learning. Copenhagen: SIKON (available from RNIB).

Nolan, C. (2002) *Under the Eye of the Clock*. New York: Arcade.

Ockelford, A. (2000) *Objects of Reference*, 3rd edn. Peterborough: RNIB.

Singer, I.B. ([1973] 1981) *A Crown of Feathers: and other stories*. New York: Farrar Straus and Giroux.

Sonksen, P.M., Levitt, S. and Kitzinger, M. (1984) Identification of constraints acting on motor development in young visually impaired children and principles of remediation, *Child Care, Health and Development*, 10: 273–86.

Spitz, R. (1945) Hospitalism: genesis of psychiatric conditions in early childhood, *Psychoanalytic Study of the Child*, 1: 53–74.

Stern, D.N. (1985) *The Interpersonal World of the Infant: A View from Psychoanalysis and Developmental Psychology*. New York: Basic Books.

Stern, D.N. (1990) *Diary of a Baby*. New York: Basic Books.

Stern, D.N. (1995) *The Motherhood Constellation*. New York: Basic Books.

Stern, D.N. (2002) *The First Relationship: Infant and Mother*. Cambridge, MA: Harvard University Press.

Stewart, I. and Joines, V. (1987) *TA Today: A New Introduction to Transactional Analysis*. Nottingham: Lifespace Publishing.

Thomas, W. and Znaniecki, F. (1996) *The Polish Peasant*. Urbana, IL: University of Illinois Press.

Trevarthen, C. (1978) Secondary intersubjectivity: confidence, confiding and acts of meaning in the first year, in A. Lock (ed.) *Action, Gesture and Symbol. The Emergence of Language*. London: Academic Press.

Trevarthen, C. (1979) Communication and cooperation in early infancy: a description of primary intersubjectivity, in M. Bullowa (ed.) *Before Speech*, pp. 321–47. New York: Cambridge University Press.

Trevarthen, C. (1999) Sharing makes sense: intersubjectivity and the making of an infant's meaning, in R. Steele and T. Treadgold (eds) *Language of Topics*. Amsterdam: Benjamins.

Webb, S. (1994) I hate plastic toys, *Nursery World*, 15: 23 December.

Winnicott, D.W. (1990) *Home is Where We Start From: Essays by a Psychoanalyst*. Harmondsworth: Penguin.

Winstock, A. (1994) *The Practical Management of Eating and Drinking Difficulties in Children*. Bicester: Winslow Press.

INDEX

DISABILITY, THE FAMILY AND SOCIETY
LISTENING TO MOTHERS

Janet Read

Circumstances dictate that many mothers play a central role in the upbringing of their disabled children. Mothers and children often find themselves involved in an unusually intimate and protracted relationship. This book explores mothers' perspectives about the ways that they find themselves acting as mediators between their children and a world that can be hostile to their interests. It takes as its starting point a study in which mothers from diverse backgrounds detail the ways in which they attempt to represent their children to the world, and the world to their children in both formal and informal interactions. They describe challenging discussions with children and other family members as well as battles and negotiations elsewhere. Their particular experiences and perspectives are linked to wider research and theory on motherhood and caring, the life patterns of disabled children and their families, and the discrimination faced by disabled children and adults.

Disability, the Family and Society will be of interest to students of disability studies, sociology, women's studies, social policy and social and community work.

Contents
Series editor's preface – Introduction – A neglected minority: an overview of policy and research – Twelve West Midlands mothers – The things that mothers do – Theorizing motherhood, mothering and caring – Living in a hostile context – Mediators and allies-on-the-ground – Index.

160pp   0 335 20310 8 (Paperback)   0 335 20311 6 (Hardback)

SPECIAL EDUCATIONAL NEEDS, INCLUSION AND DIVERSITY
A TEXTBOOK

Norah Frederickson and Tony Cline

This book has the potential to become *the* textbook on special educational needs. Written specifically with the requirements of student teachers, trainee educational psychologists, SENCO's and SEN Specialist Teachers in mind, it provides a comprehensive and detailed discussion of the major issues in special education. Whilst recognising the complex and difficult nature of many special educational needs, the authors place a firm emphasis on inclusion and suggest practical strategies enabling professionals to maximise inclusion at the same time as recognising and supporting diversity.

Key features include:

- Takes full account of linguistic, cultural and ethnic diversity unlike many other texts in the field
- Addresses the new SEN Code of Practice and is completely up to date
- Recognises current concerns over literacy and numeracy and devotes two chapters to these areas of need
- Offers comprehensive and detailed coverage of major issues in special educational needs in one volume
- Accessibly written with the needs of the student and practitioner in mind

Contents
Introduction – Part one: Principles and concepts – Children, families, schools and the wider community: an integrated approach – Concepts of special educational needs – Inclusion – Special educational needs: pathways of development – Part two: Assessment in context – Identification and assessment – Reducing bias in assessment – Curriculum based assessment – Learning environments – Part three: Areas of need – Learning difficulties – Language – Literacy – Mathematics – Hearing impairment – Emotional and behaviour difficulties – Social skills – References – Index.

528pp   0 335 20402 3 (Paperback)   0 335 20973 4 (Hardback)